Headway

Academic Skills

Reading, Writing, and Study Skills

LEVEL 3 **Teacher's Guide**

Sarah Philpot and Lesley Curnick
Series Editors: Liz and John Soars

OXFORD

Great Clarendon Street, Oxford, OX2 6DP, United Kingdom

Oxford University Press is a department of the University of Oxford. It furthers the University's objective of excellence in research, scholarship, and education by publishing worldwide. Oxford is a registered trade mark of Oxford University Press in the UK and in certain other countries

ISBN: 978 0 19 474164 4   Teacher's Guide Pack
ISBN: 978 0 19 474209 2   Teacher's Guide
ISBN: 978 0 19 474206 1   Tests CD-ROM

Printed in China

This book is printed on paper from certified and well-managed sources

ACKNOWLEDGEMENTS

Commissioned illustration by: Mark Duffin p59

The authors and publisher are grateful to those who have given permission to reproduce the following extracts and adaptations of copyright material: 1, http://www.lc.unsw. edu.ac/firststeps/differ.html; 2, http://www.insomniaeffects.net/; 7, http://middleeast.about.com/od/unitedarabemirates/qt/burj-dubai-burj-khalifa.htm

Although every effort has been made to trace and contact copyright holders before publication, this has not been possible in some cases. We apologise for any apparent infringement of copyright and, if notified, the publisher will be pleased to rectify any errors or omissions at the earliest possible opportunity.

Contents

Introduction

Headway Academic Skills

Headway Academic Skills is a multi-level course aimed at post-secondary students who need English in their academic studies. It comprises a Student's Book and Teacher's Guide for each level.

Each level consists of 10 units covering a variety of topics relevant to students in higher education. Units focus on a wide range of academic reading, writing, research, and/or vocabulary skills.

Headway Academic Skills can be used as a free-standing course, or alongside *New Headway* and *New Headway Plus*.
It can also be used as a complement to any other general English course.

Aims of *Headway Academic Skills*

The aims of *Headway Academic Skills* are to help post-secondary students become more efficient and effective in their studies by:

- developing strategies to improve reading speed, and to improve the ability to comprehend complex academic texts;
- developing strategies to produce more coherent writing, and to make clear, appropriate, and relevant notes from academic texts;
- encouraging them to adopt various approaches for dealing with new or unknown vocabulary by practising effective use of dictionaries, and through making effective vocabulary records;
- exploring and evaluating research techniques and resources, and crediting sources of information;
- promoting learner independence by encouraging students to return to earlier Study Skills to refresh their memories, or see how new skills build on and develop those previously presented.

Although the course primarily focuses on the skills of reading, writing, and research, students are given opportunities to practise their listening and speaking skills through brainstorming sessions, discussing issues, and sharing thoughts.

Ultimately, *Headway Academic Skills* also aims to develop academic skills by being transferable to all areas of students' day-to-day academic studies.

What's in the Student's Books?

Each unit of *Headway Academic Skills* LEVEL 3 consists of 7–8 hours of lessons. There are five or six sections in each unit which include Reading, Language for Writing, Writing, Research, Vocabulary Development, and Review. Each Reading, Writing, Research, and Vocabulary Development section has clear study skill aims presented in Study Skill boxes. These skills are practised through a series of controlled to freer practice exercises.

Rules boxes in the Language for Writing section highlight any grammatical areas which students may need as additional support. There is a comprehensive wordlist at the back of the book.

READING

Each reading section contains one or more texts which students use to develop different study skills. These study skills are clearly detailed in Study Skill boxes and are linked to specific practice exercises. The texts are of various types and styles which students will come across in their academic studies, including reports, articles, reviews and web pages.

LANGUAGE FOR WRITING

The language for writing section has guided writing practice including phrases and expressions for academic writing, ways of linking ideas, and relevant grammatical structures.

WRITING

Each writing section has clear outcomes for the students in terms of the type of text they may be asked to produce in other subjects, including a discursive essay, a summary, and a report using visual information. The skills covered take students through the writing process from brainstorming ideas, making notes, writing a thesis statement, selecting and organizing notes to writing and then checking their essay.

VOCABULARY DEVELOPMENT

These sections contain skills and strategies which help students develop good vocabulary learning and recording techniques. It encourages them to become more autonomous learners by making them more effective users of dictionaries, helping them to work out meanings of new words, and encouraging them to keep coherent and well-organized vocabulary records.

RESEARCH

The principal skills addressed in these sections are formulating efficient search plans, and finding and assessing reliable sources of information such as reference books and the Internet. This section also deals with the importance of recording and crediting sources in academic work.

REVIEW

The review sections give students the opportunity to reflect on skills learnt, to practise and develop them further, and to consider how these could be applied to their academic studies.

WORD LISTS

A comprehensive list of words with phonetic transcript from each unit can be found in the back of the Student's Book. Much of this vocabulary reflects the diverse vocabulary found in academic texts. It is not expected that students will learn or indeed need to learn these lists of words.

IELTS and TOEFL

Whilst this course does not deal specifically with the questions which occur in public examinations such as IELTS and TOEFL, many of the skills taught in this course have a direct application to preparing for these exams.

Headway Academic Skills Teacher's Guide

The Teacher's Guide is an easy-to-follow resource for the teacher offering step-by-step guidance to teaching *Headway Academic Skills*. As well as step-by-step procedural notes, the Teacher's Guide contains a summary of aims, lead-in tasks, background information, extension activities, and a comprehensive answer key.

Why use a Teacher's Guide?

Both the Teacher's Guides and the Student's Books have been very carefully devised in order to develop specific academic skills. As such, the treatment of materials is often different from that in a general English course. For example, pre-teaching difficult vocabulary from a text before the students read it may interfere with subsequent skills work on drawing meaning from context, or on extracting only the essential information from a complex text. Teachers are, therefore, strongly encouraged to consult the Teacher's Guide.

What's in the Teacher's Guide?

AIMS

Each reading, language for writing, writing, vocabulary development, research, and review section has a summary of the aims of that section.

LEAD IN

Lead-in activities are devised to focus students' attention on the topic and skills of each section.

PROCEDURE

Class management and step-by-step instructions.

BACKGROUND INFORMATION

These notes give teachers background information to the development of a skill, or the topic.

EXTENSION ACTIVITIES

Extension activities offer ideas on how to extend skills practice, or give students an opportunity to reflect on their learning.

ADDITIONAL PHOTOCOPIABLE ACTIVITY

There is one extra practice acivity for each unit with step-by-step instructions at the back of the Teacher's Guide.

ANSWER KEY

For ease of use, the answer key is usually on the same page as the teaching notes for each exercise, but presented separately. The answer key for each exercise is clearly referenced in the procedural notes. For example, exercise 1 key is referenced

🔑 1

We hope you and your students enjoy working with Headway Academic Skills.

1 Education and learning

READING SKILLS Effective reading (1), (2), and (3)
LANGUAGE FOR WRITING Comparing and contrasting
WRITING SKILLS Checking your writing (1) • Writing a comparing and contrasting essay
VOCABULARY DEVELOPMENT Using a dictionary (1) and (2)

READING Good study habits pp4–5

AIMS

The aims of this section are to introduce students to different reading strategies, and to help them develop good learning strategies. Students will be encouraged to reflect on how the skills presented and practised here can be applied to their other studies.

LEAD IN

- Focus students' attention on the page. Ask students to identify the skill READING, and the topic (*Good study habits*). Ask:
  – *Can anyone give us an example of a good study habit?*
- Write students' ideas on the board.

PROCEDURE

1 Students read the instructions. Students discuss answers in pairs or small groups. Ask some students to tell the class their answers. **O—1**

2 Students read the instructions. Give students 30 seconds to answer the questions. **O—2**

3 Students read the instructions and work individually to complete the task. Elicit the answers from the class. **O—3**

4 Students read the instructions and work individually to complete the task. You may wish to set a time limit (of one minute) to encourage students to scan the text for the answers rather than read intensively. Students compare their answers in pairs. Elicit the answers from the class. Do not explain the new vocabulary in bold at this stage. **O—4**

5 Students read the instructions and discuss their answers in pairs or small groups. Ask some students to describe to the class how they read the texts. **O—5**

Students read the **Study Skill**. Tell students to match the ways of reading in the **Study Skill** with their answers in exercise 5.

6 Students read the instructions and complete the task. Put students into pairs or small groups to discuss their answers. Ask some students to tell the class their answers. **O—6**

7 Students read the instructions and complete the task. Students compare answers in pairs. Elicit the answers from the class. **O—7**

8 Students read the **Study Skill**. You may want to refer students back to the **Study Skill** on p4 of the Student's Book to review skimming. Students read the instructions and complete the task. Encourage students to use their own words as far as possible to answer the questions. Ask some students to read their answers to the class. Compare the answers with the students' own ideas about good study habits from the LEAD IN. **O—8**

9 Students read the instructions. Allow students five minutes to think about how they could improve their own studies. Put students in pairs to discuss their answers. Elicit some ideas from the class. **O—9**

READING Answer key pp4–6

O—1

Students' own answers.

O—2

1 Text A
2 Text B
3 Text B

O—3

Text A	**Text B**
1 6	1 7, including introduction
2 2	2 yes
3 the results	3 no

O—4

1 a planned target
2 a cup of coffee/tea, listening to a favourite piece of music
3 watching a DVD / emails
4 allowing regular revision time

O—5

Possible answers
1 very quickly, just looked at layout and titles (survey)
2 more slowly, looked at titles, subtitles, numbering, organization of text (skim)
3 more slowly, reading bits of the text carefully (scan)

O—6

Students' own answers.

O—7

a	adjective, 7	f	verb, 8
b	adjective, 1	g	adjective, 4
c	adjective, 9	h	adjective, 10
d	noun, 5	i	verb, 3
e	adjective, 2	j	verb, 6

O—8

Possible answers
1 You can develop good study habits by having sensible targets/not planning to do too much at one time.
2 It's a good idea to tell your friends about your plans because they will know if you fail, and this will make you want to succeed.
3 If you have a small reward, you will feel good about yourself, and this will help in your studies.
4 The best time to study is when it is quiet and you are able to concentrate.
5 A large piece of work can be made easier by breaking it down into lots of smaller tasks.
6 If you keep good notes, it is easier to find the information again.
7 It is better not to leave revision until the last moment. You should try to organize regular revision time.

O—9

Students' own answers.

Education in the UK p6

LEAD IN

- Tell students to look at the title of this section. Ask:
  - *What is the UK?*
  - *What do you know about education there?*
- Put students' ideas on the board.

BACKGROUND INFORMATION

In 1707 Scotland joined England and Wales to form Great Britain (GB). The formation of the United Kingdom (UK) took place in 1801 with the inclusion of Ireland. In 1922 with the creation of the Irish Free State (the Republic of Ireland or Eire) in the south, the UK became the United Kingdom of Great Britain and Northern Ireland.

The legal school-leaving age in the UK is still 16. However, some politicians believe that the age should be raised to 18.

PROCEDURE

10 Students read the instructions and complete the task individually. If necessary, tell students to read the **Study Skill** on page 4 to remind themselves what 'skim reading' is. **○━ 10**

11 Students read the **Study Skill**. Students read the instructions and work individually to complete the task. Students compare their answers in pairs. **○━ 11**

12 Students read the instructions and work in pairs or small groups to complete the task. **○━ 12**

13 Students read the instructions and complete the task in pairs. It is important that students have the opportunity to read the text aloud in sense groups as this will help them in their comprehension. Write the paragraph on the board and ask students to mark the sense groups. Discuss their grouping with the class. Decide which grouping is best. **○━ 13**

BACKGROUND INFORMATION

Many students read a sentence word by word. This reduces their reading speed and creates problems with comprehension. Encouraging students to read in sense groups can help to overcome these problems. A sense group is a unit of words which are related by meaning and / or grammar. When reading aloud there is a pause or break before and after each sense group. There is usually no pause within a sense group. A sense group can be made up of:
- an article + adjective + noun, e.g. *The brown deer*
- a verb + adverb, e.g. *ran quickly*
- prepositional phrases, e.g. *into the forest*
- a relative clause, e.g. *which was surrounded by mountains*

14 Students read the instructions and complete the task individually. **○━ 14**

EXTENSION ACTIVITY

The number of words in the text is given at the end of the text. To encourage your students to increase their reading speed, tell them to work out what their average reading speed is. To do this, they should:
- choose a text, either from their area of academic study or from this course
- count the number of words
- time how long it takes them to read the text
- divide the number of words by the time taken, e.g. 900 words in four minutes = 225wpm (words per minute)
- repeat the process
- average the two results, e.g. 1) 225wpm 2) 205wpm = average reading speed of 215wpm

Encourage students to time themselves with the texts in this course.

○━ 10
1 B
2 A
3 D
4 C
5 E

○━ 11
1 The <u>school year runs</u> from <u>September</u> to <u>July</u> and is usually <u>divided</u> into <u>three terms</u> of approximately <u>13 weeks</u> each.
2 These <u>schools</u> are largely <u>co-educational</u>, that is, <u>boys</u> and <u>girls</u> attend <u>together</u>.
3 Most <u>students</u> go to large <u>comprehensive schools</u> which <u>teach children</u> of <u>varying abilities</u>.

○━ 12
1 no
2 middle school
3 60%

○━ 13
Possible answers
By law in the UK / all children between 5 and 16 years of age / must receive a full-time education. / The vast majority, / over 90%, of these children / attend state schools. / The education systems in Wales, Northern Ireland, and England / are similar, / whereas the education system in Scotland differs / in a number of ways. / This description will generally refer to / the English state system.

○━ 14
1 C
2 D, E
3 A (only the introduction as this tells the reader that Scotland is not described.)

LANGUAGE FOR WRITING p7
Comparing and contrasting

AIMS
The aim of this section is help students to recognize and use fixed phrases and linking words that are commonly used in academic writing.

PROCEDURE

1 Students read the instructions and discuss the expressions in pairs or small groups. Elicit the answers from the class. **⊙₁ 1**

2 Students read the instructions and complete the task individually. Write the sentences on the board. Ask some students to come to the board and underline the words and phrases that show a similarity or difference. **⊙₁ 2**

3 Students read the instructions and complete the task individually. Write the table on the board and ask some students to add the phrases to it. **⊙₁ 3**

Ask:
– *Which words or phrases are followed by a comma?* (In the same way / on the other hand / in contrast)
– *Which words or phrases are preceded by a comma?* (whereas / on the other hand   when they are used in the second clause of a sentence)

4 Students read the instructions and complete the task individually. Put students into pairs to compare answers. **⊙₁ 4**

5 Students read the instructions and complete the task individually. Tell students to complete the sentences, using information about the education system in their own country plus their own ideas. Ask some students to read out their answers. **⊙₁ 5**

ADDITIONAL PHOTOCOPIABLE ACTIVITY

Writing 1 Comparing and contrasting

LANGUAGE FOR WRITING Answer key p7

⊙₁ 1

Whereas shows that things are different.
In the same way shows that things are similar.

⊙₁ 2

1 The school year in the UK runs from September to July. In Australia, <u>on the other hand</u>, students go to school from late January to December.
2 <u>Both</u> Sweden <u>and</u> France have a compulsory national curriculum.
3 Japanese schools <u>are different from</u> schools in many other countries <u>in that</u> they usually have an entrance exam.
4 Malaysian schools have two terms a year. <u>In contrast</u>, Australian schools have four terms.
5 School students all over the world <u>are similar in that</u> they have to take exams.

⊙₁ 3

similar	different
In the same way	whereas
Both … and	on the other hand
are similar in that	are different from … in that
	In contrast

⊙₁ 4

1 **Both** Wales **and** Ireland include their own language in the curriculum.
2 State and private schools **are similar in that** all their students take school-leaving exams.
3 Northern Ireland and Wales have a similar education system to England. Scotland, **on the other hand**, has its own system.
4 In the UK, education is compulsory for children to the age of 16, **whereas** in Brazil children can leave school at 14.
5 Students in Japanese schools often eat school lunches. **In the same way**, students in France also often eat in school.

⊙₁ 5

Students' own answers.

WRITING
Education in Japan and England: a comparison pp8–9

AIMS
The aim of this section is to guide students through the process of writing a comparing and contrasting essay, using the appropriate expressions from *Language for Writing*.

LEAD IN
- Tell students to look at the title of this section (Education in Japan and England: a comparison). Ask:
  – *Has anyone been to Japan?*
  – *What do you know about education in Japan?*
- Write students' ideas on the board.

PROCEDURE

1 Students read the instructions and individually write a list of three things they remember about the UK education system. Put the students into pairs (or small groups) to compare their lists and to discuss what is similar and what is different about the education system in their own country. Ask some pairs or groups to tell the class their ideas. **○── 1**

2 Students read the instructions and work individually to complete the task. Ask some students to tell the class what headings they used. **○── 2**

3 Students read the instructions and complete the task. Ask some students to write their questions on the board. The rest of the class compare their own questions with those on the board. **○── 3**

4 Students read the instructions and work in pairs (or small groups) to complete the task. Tell students they can use their own questions from exercise 3, or choose the questions on the board. Students write their answers in the table.

Ask some pairs or groups to tell the rest of the class about their notes.

5 Students read the **Study Skill**. Students read the instructions and complete the task individually. Write the long sentences on the board. Ask students to come to the board and show the rest of the class how they divided the sentences. Discuss other students' answers. **○── 5**

6 Students read the instructions and complete the task individually. Put students in pairs to compare their answers. Ask some students to tell the rest of the class their answers. Students compare these with their own answers. **○── 6**

7 Students read the instructions and complete the task. Put students in pairs to compare their answers. **○── 7**

Writing a comparing and contrasting essay p9

8 Students read the instructions. You may wish to set the essay writing for homework. Tell students to write or type their essay double spaced (a clean line between each written line) as this will make correcting errors much easier.

9 Students read the instructions and check their essay. You may wish to introduce the idea of peer correction. Explain to students that peer correction is an opportunity to help fellow students to improve their writing and should be helpful rather than critical. Students exchange essays and check their colleague's essay for sentence length, missing words, and the use of linking words and phrases.

EXTENSION ACTIVITY

Tell students to select an essay that they have written for their academic studies. Tell them to bring the essay to class and exchange essays for peer correction.

Or tell students to re-read their own essay and to check for sentence length, missing words, and the use of linking words and phrases.

WRITING Answer key pp8–9

○── 1 Students' own answers.

○── 2
Possible answers
1 General information
2 School timetable/School year
3 Primary school
4 Secondary school
5 Examinations

○── 3
Possible answers
1 General information
   When is school compulsory?
   What percentage of students go to state schools?
2 School year
   When does the school year start and finish?
   How many terms are there?
   When does a school day start and finish?
   What do schoolchildren do for lunch?
3 Primary school
   When do children attend primary school?
   Are boys and girls taught together?
   What subjects do they study?
4 Secondary school
   What type of schools do children go to?
   At what age do students start and finish secondary school?
5 Examinations
   When do students take exams?
   What do students need to go to university?

○── 5
Possible answers
By law, Japanese children have to attend school from the age of 6 to 15. On the other hand, English children start compulsory school at the age of 5 and continue until they are 16.

The Japanese and English education systems are similar in that it is necessary to take an exam to enter university. However, Japan is different from England because each university sets its own entrance exam, whereas all English universities accept students with good A level results.

○── 6
Possible answers
1 The Japanese school year starts in April, whereas the English school year starts in September.
2 Both English and Japanese schools have three terms. English and Japanese schools are similar in that they have three terms.
3 Japanese students eat a school lunch, whereas many English students take food to school for lunch.

○── 7
The school systems in Japan and England <u>are similar</u> in that students have to take exams. However, <u>in</u> Japan each school can set entrance exams. <u>In contrast</u>, English schools do <u>not usually</u> have entrance exams. At the end of their time <u>at</u> school, students in both countries have <u>to take</u> exams to enter university. There are places for everyone with the right qualifications, but very good grades are required to get into the best universities in both countries. Although there are a number of significant differences between the systems, both countries share a commitment to high quality education for their young people.

○── 8
Students' own answers.

VOCABULARY DEVELOPMENT Dictionary work p10

AIMS
The aim of this section is to make students aware of how a dictionary can help with their studies in English, especially with the correct use of vocabulary.

LEAD IN
- Ask students to brainstorm what information an English–English dictionary gives about a word. Put their ideas on the board. ▶▶ **Lead in**

PROCEDURE

1 Students read the **Study Skill**. You may wish to advise students to buy or borrow a good English–English dictionary and encourage them to bring it to class.

Students read the instructions. Check that students understand what a *syllable* is (a word or part of a word which contains one vowel sound). Students work individually to complete the task. Put students in pairs to compare answers. Ask some students to tell the class their answers. **⊶ 1**

2 Students read the instructions and complete the task individually. Elicit the answers from the class. **⊶ 2**

3 Tell students to read the **Study Skill**. Tell them that it is important to look at the example sentences in a dictionary entry to get information on how to *use* words correctly.

Students read the instructions and complete the task individually. Put students into pairs to compare answers. **⊶ 3**

4 Students read the instructions and work individually to complete the task. You may wish to tell your students that the mistakes concern the grammar patterns of the underlined verbs. Write the sentences on the board. Ask some students to come to the board and correct the mistakes. **⊶ 4**

EXTENSION ACTIVITY
Students work in pairs or small groups. Each pair or group selects five words from the texts in this unit.

Students use their dictionaries to write four or five questions (like those in exercise 1) about their words.

Ask each pair or group to write their word and questions on the board. The rest of the class use their dictionaries to answer the questions.

For example:
lecture
1 How many syllables are there in this word? (2)
2 Which syllable has the main stress? (first)
3 What part of speech is it? (noun and verb)
4 How many meanings does it have? (2)
5 What prepositions are used with it? (on/about)

VOCABULARY DEVELOPMENT Answer key p10

▶▶ Lead in
Possible answers
meaning, pronunciation, example sentences, part of speech, etc.

⊶ 1
1 3
2 the first
3 a noun
4 dictionaries
5 2

⊶ 2
1 a noun
2 2
3 on the first syllable
4 lean
5 leapfrog/learning
6 leant or leaned
7 learnt or learned

⊶ 3
1 This master's degree consists **of** six modules.
2 There are many scholarships available **to/for** overseas students.
3 Education in most countries is funded mainly **by** the state.
4 The Internet is a good source **of** information.
5 If you wish to apply **to** a university, you should prepare your application carefully.

⊶ 4
1 The university lets students ~~to~~ use dictionaries in their exams.
2 Students are encouraged ~~joining~~ **to join** university societies.
3 Students are expected **to** hand in their work on time.
4 Please speak **to** your tutor if you have any problems.
5 Students usually sit ~~on~~ their exams in June.

REVIEW p11

AIMS

The aims of this section are to give students further practice in the skills learnt in this unit, and to give them the opportunity to review the work they have done. A further aim is to encourage students to apply what they have learnt to their academic studies in English.

PROCEDURE

1 Students read the instructions. Put students into pairs or small groups to answer the questions. Elicit answers from the class. If students produce different answers, ask them to give examples to support them. **o⟶ 1**

2 Students read the instructions and work individually to complete the task. Ask some students to write their answers on the board. Discuss these with the class and ask for other possibilities. **o⟶ 2**

3 Students read the **Study Skill**. Remind students of the importance of accuracy in written work. Students read the instructions and complete the task individually. Put students in pairs or small groups to compare their answers. Write the paragraph on the board and ask some students to come to the board and put in the corrections. **o⟶ 3**

4 Students read the instructions and work individually to complete the task. Ask some students to write the answers on the board. The rest of the class compare their answers. **o⟶ 4**

5 Students read the instructions and work individually to complete the task. Put students into pairs to compare answers. **o⟶ 5**

EXTENSION ACTIVITY

Ask the students to list the skills they have learnt and practised in this unit. For example:
– how to read effectively (skim, scan, and read intensively)
– how to read faster
– how to check written work
– how to get information from a dictionary

Encourage them to apply these skills to the work they do in their academic studies.

REVIEW Answer key p11

o⟶ 1

Possible answers
1 scan
2 skim
3 scan and read intensively
4 read intensively
5 scan and read intensively

o⟶ 2

Possible answers
1 You will need to read a difficult text several times.
2 Japanese students go to school for seven hours a day.
3 A typical university course lasts three or four years.
4 Students often use the Internet to get information.

o⟶ 3

Here to help!
Are you a new student? In your first few days at university you will need to register for your classes, and find out where and when they are held. You will also meet many new people, students, lecturers, and other members of the university staff. You will certainly be given long lists of books that are required reading for your course, as well as a list of essays and other course assignments.
All of this can be very daunting and stressful. But don't worry, we are here to help you. The Students' Advisory Group (SAG) is available to answer your questions, show you around the university, and to help with any other problems.
Come to our office in Room 501, 5th floor, Central Building, or ask any student wearing a SAG badge. And good luck with your studies!

o⟶ 4

chemistry
1 noun
2 stress on first syllable
3 n/a
4 no plural form; it is an uncountable noun

ability
1 noun
2 stress on second syllable
3 n/a
4 abilities

compulsory
1 adjective
2 stress on second syllable
3 n/a
4 n/a

apply
1 verb
2 stress on second syllable
3 applied, applied
4 n/a

tertiary
1 adjective
2 stress on first syllable
3 n/a
4 n/a

choose
1 verb
2 one syllable
3 chose, chosen
4 n/a

o⟶ 5

1 chose/applied	4 tertiary
2 compulsory	5 applied
3 abilities	6 chemistry

2 Innovations in health and medicine

READING SKILLS Predicting content • Topic sentences • Avoiding plagiarism (1)
LANGUAGE FOR WRITING Rephrasing
WRITING SKILLS Developing a paragraph • Writing a paragraph
VOCABULARY DEVELOPMENT Recording vocabulary (1), (2), and (3)

READING A musical cure pp12–13

AIMS
The aims of this section are to give students practice in predicting the content of texts from pictures and titles, identifying and using topic sentences, and understanding how plagiarism can be avoided.

LEAD IN
• Focus students' attention on the page. Ask students to identify the skill READING, and the topic (*A musical cure*). Ask students to tell you what cures they know for illnesses (drugs, painkillers, etc.). If they don't know the word *cure*, help them by saying an aspirin is a cure for a headache, etc.

PROCEDURE

1 Students read the instructions. Students discuss their answers in pairs or small groups for two minutes. Elicit answers from the class. **⊶ 1**

2 Tell students to read the **Study Skill**. Students read the instructions and answer the questions. Students compare their answers in pairs. **⊶ 2**

3 Students focus on the title of the text. Ask students to explain *healing* (making someone healthy again) and *therapy* (treatment for an illness, sometimes without drugs). Students read the instructions. Students focus on the example given. Students write one question for each question word. Write some students' questions on the board. **⊶ 3**

4 Students read the instructions and complete the task. Get students to work in pairs to compare answers. Go back to students' questions on the board from exercise 3. Ask:
 – *Have your questions been answered?* **⊶ 4**

5 Students read the **Study Skill** and the instructions. Focus students' attention on the example given. Elicit why that is the topic sentence (it gives the subject of the paragraph, which is then expanded on). Students complete the task. Students work in pairs to compare answers. **⊶ 5**

6 Students read the instructions and complete the task. **⊶ 6**

7 Students read the instructions and complete the task, answering the questions in exercise 6. Ask if students' predictions in exercise 2 were correct. **⊶ 7**

8 Students read the instructions and focus on the example. Elicit the three main points in the topic sentence ('has long been used', 'treat', and 'different problems') Elicit which highlighted information in paragraph 2 corresponds to those points.

 Has long been used: ancient Greeks, both world wars, currently

 treat: healing properties

 different problems: people – trauma, cancer, Alzheimer's, long-term pain, learning disabilities

 Students complete the task. **⊶ 8** p13

READING Answer key pp12–14

⊶ 1
Possible answers
Where: at home, when travelling, at concerts, in the street, etc.
When: at all times of day and night, when tired, when relaxing, etc.
Why: to entertain, to relax, to study, etc.

⊶ 2
1 a newspaper or magazine
2 a patient in hospital listening to a CD player/walkman; a musician (harpist) playing in a hospital ward
3 b general readers

⊶ 3
Possible answers
Where is music used as a therapy?
How is music used as a therapy? How long has music been used? How does it work?
What is it used to treat?
Who did the study?

⊶ 4
Where? Music used as a therapy in ancient Greece; study carried out in London
How? Patients listen to a performance; used since ancient times, e.g. during world wars; improves general well-being; maybe electrical messages are sent to the brain
What? Many different diseases, e.g. cancer, Alzheimer's, long-term pain, learning disabilities
Who? Study was carried out in Chelsea and Westminster hospital in London, funded by Wellcome Trust

⊶ 5
2 Music has long been used to treat patients suffering from different problems.
3 There is growing evidence that music can cause physical changes to the body which can improve our health.
4 These very positive results are partly due to general well-being.
5 Music has other effects which have not yet been understood.
6 Science, however, demands facts and hard evidence.

⊶ 6
2 Paragraph 2   4 Paragraphs 4 and 5
3 Paragraph 3   5 Paragraph 4

⊶ 7
Possible answers
1 Up till now reports have been based mainly on anecdotal evidence. These new studies could provide that proof.
2 It is used for many different diseases such as cancer, Alzheimer's, long-term pain, and learning disabilities.
3 Stress levels were reduced, recovery times were improved, and fewer drugs were needed.
4 The effects are partly due to a feeling of well-being. Music increases feelings of joy. It is also suggested that music stimulates the brain to be active and to send electrical messages to muscles and limbs.
5 People feel better and recover from disease more quickly.

A new vaccine p14

LEAD IN

- Write on the board the title of the page: *A new vaccine*. Ask:
  - *What are vaccines used for?* (to protect people from developing diseases)
  - *What are they?* (injections of a mild form of the disease)
  - *What vaccinations have you had?* (polio, diptheria, tetanus)
  - *When do people have vaccinations?* (in childhood, or before travelling to certain countries)

PROCEDURE

9 Students read the instructions. Students discuss the answers in pairs or in small groups. Write students' answers on the board. ⊶ 9

10 Students read the instructions. Students work in pairs or small groups and discuss the possible topic of each paragraph. Ask some pairs or groups to tell the class their ideas. Write some of these ideas on the board. Do not worry if they are contradictory at this stage. ⊶ 10

11 Students read the instructions. Students check if the predictions from exercises 9 and 10 written on the board were right.

12 Students read the instructions. Ask:

- *How do you scan read?*

If necessary, refer students to the **Study Skill** on p4. Students discuss the answers in pairs or small groups. ⊶ 12

13 Students read the instructions. Students discuss the answers in pairs or in small groups. ⊶ 13

14 Students read the **Study Skill** and the instructions. Students discuss the answers in pairs or in small groups. ⊶ 14

EXTENSION ACTIVITY

Get students to re-read the text and to underline any new vocabulary. Tell students to use an English–English dictionary to look up these words.

Do **not** teach or explain new vocabulary at this stage. Tell students to make a record of these words.

⊶ 8

Paragraph 3: There is <u>growing evidence</u> that music can <u>cause physical changes</u> to the body which can <u>improve our health</u>. In <u>the Wellcome Trust study</u>, which took place over three years at the Chelsea and Westminster hospital in London, patients were asked to listen to musical performances. As a result, it was found that <u>stress levels were significantly reduced</u>, <u>recovery times were improved</u>, and <u>fewer drugs were needed</u>.

Paragraph 4: <u>These very positive results</u> are partly due to <u>general well-being</u>. It is already accepted that when <u>people feel happy</u> and have a <u>positive approach to life</u>, they are <u>more likely to feel better</u> and <u>recover from disease quickly</u>. Music <u>increases this feeling of joy</u> and <u>adds to the recovery process</u>.

Paragraph 5: However, not all these benefits can be attributed to an increase in well-being. Music has <u>other effects</u> which <u>have not yet been understood</u>. According to Professor Robertson, a scientist and musician, <u>some effects of music are mysterious</u> and are, therefore, being investigated further. It has been suggested that the <u>sounds and rhythms of music help stimulate the brain</u> and <u>send electrical messages to the muscles and limbs</u>.

Paragraph 6: Science, however, demands facts and hard evidence. Many in the medical profession have <u>not yet recognized the healing benefits of music</u>, since <u>reports</u> have been <u>based mainly on anecdotal evidence</u>. These <u>new studies could provide proof</u> to medical practitioners that <u>music is a suitable treatment for many conditions</u>. One day <u>doctors may</u> even 'prescribe' music, but that could be <u>a long time in the future</u>.

⊶ 9

Possible answers
A study has been done on a new treatment for cancer. The results are promising. The article explains the study and the results.

⊶ 10

Possible answers
Paragraph A: A vaccine has been developed which has cured lung cancer.
Paragraph B: People involved in the trials were in the early and advanced stages of the disease. The disease did not spread.
Paragraph C: The vaccine stimulates the immune system to deal with the harmful cancer/cells.
Paragraph D: Further studies will be carried out.

⊶ 12

1F 2T 3F 4F 5T 6T

⊶ 13

The vocabulary and the sentence structures are different. The summary is shorter and gives only the main points.

⊶ 14

fewer than fifty people = forty-three patients
their own vaccine = it is made specifically for each patient
which activated this body's immune system = it stimulates the body's immune system
enabled it to fight the cancer = attacks and destroys them
other forms of cancer can be cured in a similar way = it offers great hope for the treatment of cancer in general

LANGUAGE FOR WRITING   Rephrasing   p15

AIMS

The aim of this section is to help students to recognize and use fixed phrases and linking words which are commonly used in academic writing.

PROCEDURE

1 Students read the instructions. Students work individually and then discuss the answers in pairs or in small groups. **⊶ 1**

BACKGROUND INFORMATION

A synonym is a word or phrase that has the same meaning as another word or phrase. However, not all synonyms can be used in the same context. A near synonym is a word or phrase that has a <u>similar</u> meaning to another word or phrase. A near synonym can be used in fewer contexts than a true synonym.

2 Students read the instructions. Students work individually and then discuss the answers in pairs or in small groups. Ask some students to write their sentences on the board. The rest of the class compares their answers. **⊶ 2**

3 Students read the instructions and the **Rules**. Students work individually and then discuss their answers in pairs or in small groups. **⊶ 3**

4 Students read the instructions. Students work individually and then discuss their answers in pairs or in small groups. **⊶ 4**

5 Students read the instructions. Students work individually and then discuss their sentences on the board. The rest of the class compares their answers. **⊶ 5**

ADDITIONAL PHOTOCOPIABLE ACTIVITY

Writing 2 Rephrasing

LANGUAGE FOR WRITING   Answer key   p15

⊶ 1

1 researchers/scientists, carried out/conducted, trials/tests
2 study/research, results/findings, promising/encouraging
3 disease/illness, were cured/recovered

⊶ 2

2 Although the research was limited to fewer than fifty people, the findings were very encouraging.
3 Some of the patients at an advanced stage of the illness recovered.

⊶ 3

2 The funding for the study was provided by the government.
3 Alternative therapies have been used for many years (by doctors).
4 Their/Scientists' theories are usually tested in the laboratory.
5 Their/The researchers' findings will be published next month.

⊶ 4

1 a The ‖main‖ causes of ‖acute‖ asthma attacks are common cold viruses.
  b Common cold viruses are the ‖principal‖ causes of ‖severe‖ asthma attacks.
2 a Scientists use radiation to ‖investigate‖ details of ‖tiny‖ structures.
  b Scientists use radiation to ‖study‖ details of ‖very small‖ structures.
3 a A short ‖ten-minute walk‖ ‖every day‖ can be ‖beneficial to‖ your health.
  b ‖Walking for ten minutes‖ ‖daily‖ can ‖benefit‖ your health.

⊶ 5

Possible answers
1 Evidence is needed that the treatment is/drugs are effective.
2 An enormous medical centre will be built soon.
3 Many illnesses are caused by an unhealthy way of life.
4 The talk was cancelled because the speaker/presenter was unwell/ill.

WRITING Keeping healthy pp16–17

AIMS

The aim of this section is to give students practice in paragraph writing, including topic sentences, body sentences, and final sentences. Students will write a paragraph about vaccinations and the prevention of diseases.

LEAD IN

- Write *Keeping Healthy* on the board and ask:
  - *What is good for your health?*
  - *What is bad for your health?*
- Write students' ideas on the board.

PROCEDURE

1 Students read the instructions and discuss the questions in pairs or small groups. Elicit answers from the students. Students compare their answers with the ideas on the board. **⊶ 1**

2 Students read the **Study Skill**. Students read the instructions and work individually. Remind students that a topic sentence gives the subject of the paragraph. Students compare their answers in pairs or small groups. Ask some students to write their sentences on the board. Discuss which sentences are best and why. **⊶ 2**

3 Students read the instructions and complete the task individually. Students compare their answers in pairs or small groups. **⊶ 3**

4 Students read the instructions and complete the task individually. Students compare their answers in pairs or small groups. **⊶ 4**

5 Students read the instructions and complete the task individually. Students compare their answers in pairs or small groups. **⊶ 5**

6 Students read the instructions and complete the task individually. Students compare their answers in pairs or small groups. Ask some students to write their sentences on the board. Discuss which sentences are best and why. **⊶ 6**

Writing a paragraph p17

7 Students read the instructions and complete the task individually. **⊶ 7**

EXTENSION ACTIVITY

Remind students that checking their work is important.

Either tell students to check their own work for topic sentence, body sentences and final sentence, or put students into pairs to check each other's work for these things.

WRITING Answer key pp16–17

⊶ 1

Possible answers
1 once a year for a check-up, or only when you are ill
2 by eating a well-balanced diet and taking exercise
3 a mixture of all types of food, such as proteins, carbohydrates, fats, fibre, vitamins and minerals; not too much sugar or fat; lots of fruit and vegetables

⊶ 2

Possible answers
B It is important for everyone to drink enough water every day.
C A well-balanced diet is essential to keep healthy.

⊶ 3

1 We should all eat five portions of fruit and vegetables a day, according to nutritionists. **a** It has been proved that eating regular amounts of fresh fruit and vegetables reduces the risk of developing serious diseases. **d** It is easy to follow these guidelines by having fruit juice for breakfast and vegetables with your main course at lunch, followed by a piece of fruit for dessert. **f** If you then include salad or more vegetables with your evening meal, you will soon reach the target five portions.
2 Obesity is a growing problem all over the world. **b** In some developed countries, over 50% of the population is overweight. **c** This is in part due to an unhealthy diet, but also to lack of exercise. **e** There is also growing concern over the number of young people who suffer from weight problems.

⊶ 4

Model answer
1 The weather can affect how people feel. It has been shown that people who live in countries where the days are very short in the winter, with little sunlight, suffer from depression. However, those who live in sunny countries are less likely to have mental health problems. Generally, sunshine improves our mood.

⊶ 5

1 C 2 A 3 B

⊶ 6

Possible answers
Antibiotics: It is, therefore, important that antibiotics are not prescribed unnecessarily.
Back pain: It is always important, however, to consult a doctor if you suffer from long periods of back pain.

⊶ 7

Students' own answers.

VOCABULARY DEVELOPMENT
Recording vocabulary p18

AIMS
The aim of this section is to help students make choices about what new vocabulary to record and how to record it.

LEAD IN
- Ask:
  - *What words do you record?*
  - *Do you record every new word?*
  - *Do you write down the same information about every new word?*
- Write students' answers on the board. Explain that not every word is useful to every student. It depends on their needs. For example, an engineering student will need more technical words than a history student. Tell students they should think about whether the words are important for their studies.

PROCEDURE
1 Tell students to read the **Study Skill**. Elicit what *key words* are (important words or phrases related to the topic), and focus on the fact that the words students record should be ones they will need to use when they write or to search through indexes or electronic sources. Students work in pairs or small groups to complete the task. **⊶ 1**

2 Students read the **Study Skill**. Write a word on the board (e.g. *write*). Elicit the different information about *write* that is listed in the **Study Skill**:
  - pronunciation /raɪt/
  - part of speech: verb
  - irregular forms: wrote, written
  - associated prepositions: to write **to** someone, **about** something, to write something **down**
  - example sentence: I wrote an essay last week.
  - definition: to make words on paper using a pen or pencil

  Students read the instructions. Elicit the meaning of *active use* (to be used in writing or speaking, not just to be understood). Students complete the task individually. Students compare their answers with a partner. Compare this with students' answers from the LEAD IN. **⊶ 2**

3 Tell students to read the **Study Skill**. Ask:
  - *What methods of recording vocabulary do you use?*
  - *Do you know any other methods?* (according to topic, in lists, in a mind map, on note cards, on a computer).

  Elicit why it is better to record words according to topic than alphabetically listing words from a lesson (words are easier to retrieve and remember if they are organized according to topic). Students read the instructions. Students work in pairs and complete the task. **⊶ 3**

4 Students read the instructions. Students work individually and complete the task. Students compare their answers with a partner. **⊶ 4**

EXTENSION ACTIVITY
Tell students to look at the vocabulary they recorded for the extension activity on p13 of the Teacher's Guide. Tell them to go through the vocabulary and choose a maximum of ten words they would like to record for active use. Students use a dictionary to find the information they need about each word. Students choose an appropriate method to record the words.

VOCABULARY DEVELOPMENT Answer key p18

⊶ 1
1 a literature student: novel, author
2 a medical student: heal, therapy, immune, vaccine, disease
3 all students: curriculum, data, analyse, grading, define, course, lecture

⊶ 2
1 active use: suffer, cut
2 understanding only: prestigious, intake

⊶ 3
1 according to topic
2 mind map
3 a group of words with similar meaning

⊶ 4
scientists, geneticists, physicists, biologists, chemists (as a mind map or according to topic)
food, proteins, fats, minerals, vitamins, sugars, carbohydrates (as a mind map or according to topic)
encouraging, favourable, promising, positive (as a group of words with similar meanings)

REVIEW p19

AIMS

The aims of this section are to give students further practice in the skills learnt in this unit, and to give them the opportunity to review the work they have done. A further aim is to encourage students to apply what they have learnt to their academic studies in English.

PROCEDURE

1 Students read the instructions. Students work in pairs or small groups and complete the task. 🔑 1

BACKGROUND INFORMATION

There are some sayings in English about certain food being good for you. For example:

Carrots help you see in the dark (traditionally used to encourage children to eat carrots).

An apple a day keeps the doctor away.

2 Students read the instructions and complete the task. 🔑 2

3 Students read the instructions and complete the task individually. Students compare answers with a partner. 🔑 3

4 Students read the instructions. Remind students to change the vocabulary and the grammar in the sentences. Students complete the task individually. Ask some students to write their answers on the board. Discuss which are best and why. 🔑 4

5 Elicit from students the different types of sentences found in a paragraph (topic, body, and final). Students read the instructions and complete the task. 🔑 5

6 Ask students to recall how to choose which words to record and the methods of recording vocabulary:
– words that will be useful to them
– as mind maps, in topic lists, words with similar meanings

Students work alone to make their vocabulary records. 🔑 6

EXTENSION ACTIVITY

Ask the students to list the skills they have learnt and practised in this unit. For example:
– predicting the content of texts
– recognizing and writing topic sentences
– rephrasing to avoid plagiarism
– organizing a paragraph
– recording vocabulary

Put students into small groups to discuss how they could apply these skills to their other academic studies.

Tell students to select vocabulary from texts they are reading in their other academic studies and to record them using one or more of the methods practised in this unit. You could ask students to present these vocabulary groups to the class.

This activity could be set as homework.

REVIEW Answer key p19

🔑 1

1 a newspaper or magazine
2 probably the general reader
3 vegetables (carrots, peas, broccoli) and a woman having her eyes examined/tested
4 Carrots improve your eyesight or help you see at night.

🔑 2

1 B 2 C 3 A

🔑 3

1 older people
2 It reduces the chances.
3 It causes loss of clear, sharp vision.
4 The consumption of coloured vegetables was monitored in a group of women between the ages of 50 and 79. The study took 15 years.

🔑 4

Possible answers
1 The risk of developing the illness can be reduced by increasing the intake of these vegetables.
2 A study group was headed by Dr Suzan Moeller.
3 They recorded the women's intake of coloured vegetables over 15 years.
4 An increased consumption of these vegetables lowered the risk of developing the disease in women under 75.

🔑 5

Students' own answers.

🔑 6

Students' own answers.

3 Urban planning

READING SKILLS Paragraph purpose • Text cohesion
RESEARCH Using reference material • Searching the Internet efficiently (1) and (2)
WRITING SKILLS Selecting information • Prioritizing • Brainstorming • Writing a persuasive article
VOCABULARY DEVELOPMENT Collocations (1)

READING A model of good urban planning pp20–21

AIMS
The aims of this section are to show students how to identify the purpose of paragraphs within a text, and to recognize how ideas are connected from one paragraph to another.

LEAD IN
• Focus students' attention on the page. Ask students to identify the skill READING, and the topic (*A model of good urban planning*). Ask:
  – *Who is responsible for organizing and planning towns and cities?*
  – *What sort of things are involved in town planning?* (roads, water supply, etc.)
• Put students' ideas on the board.

PROCEDURE
1 Students read the instructions and discuss the questions in pairs. Ask some students to tell the rest of the class their answers. **○┑ 1**

2 Students read the instructions and complete the task. If necessary, remind students what *survey* means or tell them to re-read the **Study Skill** on page 4. Setting a time limit, e.g. 30 seconds, may encourage students to survey more efficiently. **○┑ 2**

3 Students read the instructions and skim the text. Students compare their answers in pairs. **○┑ 3**

4 Students read the instructions and complete the task. Elicit the answers from the class. **○┑ 4**

5 Students read the **Study Skill** and the instructions. Students work individually to complete the task and then compare their answers in pairs or small groups. **○┑ 5**

6 Tell students to read the **Study Skill**. Allow students some time to read about the different ways of showing continuity of ideas. Clarify that 'maintaining the grammatical subject' does not mean the same as keeping the same topic.

  Students read the instructions. Put students in pairs to complete the task. If possible, prepare the text so that it can be projected on the board. Elicit the answers from the class or ask some students to come up and mark the connecting language on the OHT. **○┑ 6**

7 Students read the instructions. Tell them to look at the language which was underlined and to match it with a method in the second column. Students work in pairs to complete the task. Elicit the answers from the class. **○┑ 7**

8 Students read the instructions and complete the task individually. Tell students to make notes for their answers. **○┑ 8** p19

READING Answer key pp20–22

○┑ 1 Students' own answers.

○┑ 2 1 a professional journal 2 a view of the city / public transport 3 Curitiba

○┑ 3 1 yes (to a certain extent) 2 no 3 yes (to a certain extent) 4 yes

○┑ 4 1 in southern Brazil 2 in the 1940s 3 almost 1 million 4 yes

○┑ 5 1 H 2 C, D, E, F 3 G 4 B 5 A

○┑ 6
A This review will argue … the type of urban planning found in Curitiba is more important than ever.
B As stated in the introduction, Curitiba is a fine example of how urban planning can work. … How, then, did Curitiba address these problems?
C By the 1940s, … Consequently, they employed a French planner and architect, Alfred Agache, to find an overall solution.
D Agache studied all aspects of the problem. … The result, as described below, was that his scheme only served Curitiba for another 20 years.
E By the 1960s, … It is clear that the Curitiba Master Plan was one of the first attempts to integrate all aspects of city planning.
F This integrated approach to urban design was maintained … However, good transportation remained central to the planning.
G Good transportation still remains a priority, … but its city planners are continually searching for solutions to the problems.
H It is apparent that, as an increasing number of people move into cities, the challenges for urban planners will also grow. …

○┑ 7
a paragraphs A–B (3) a backward reference (as stated in the introduction)
b paragraphs B–C (4) a question (How, then, did Curitiba address these problems?)
c paragraphs C–D (5) repeating key word (… Alfred Agache, to find an overall solution. / Agache studied …)
d paragraphs D–E (6) a forward reference (as described below)
e paragraphs E–F (1) rephrasing key words (… to integrate all aspects of city planning. / This integrated approach to urban design …)
f paragraphs F–G (2) maintaining the subject (Good transportation remained … / Good transportation still remains …)

A capital city p22

LEAD IN

- Put students into pairs or small groups. Each group chooses a secretary. Tell them they will have one minute to write down the names of as many capital cities as they can. At the end of the time, ask the group that has the most names to write them on the board for the class to check.

PROCEDURE

9 Students read the instructions. Ask:
  – *How are you going to read the text?* (skim)

  Students skim the text to identify the first paragraph and answer the questions. Students compare their answers in pairs. **⊙━ 9**

10 Students read the instructions. You may want them to re-read the **Study Skill** on p20 to remind them of the language that shows connections between paragraphs. Students compare their answers in pairs or small groups, and analyse the method used to show continuity of ideas from one paragraph to another. The language showing continuity is underlined in the answers. **⊙━ 10**

11 Students read the instructions and complete the task individually. Students compare answers in pairs. Ask some students to tell the class their answers. **⊙━ 11**

EXTENSION ACTIVITY

Tell students to read the text again and to select between five and ten items of vocabulary that may be useful to them.

Remind them of the importance of recording such vocabulary:
– so that they can find it again easily
– with the information (irregular forms, pronunciation, etc.) they will need to use it correctly in their writing or speaking

⊙━ 8

Possible answers (note form)
1 physical, economic, and social development
2 growing rapidly so overcrowding, pollution, growing demand for services, transport, and housing
3 immigration from Japan, Syria, and Lebanon – workers for agriculture and industry
4 Agache looked at all aspects of the problem – not just one.
5 it wasn't completed
6 added wide, fast roads, reduced city growth, reduced traffic, preserved historic centre – integrated approach
7 environmental concerns, so a recycling programme introduced, parks built, 'green' spaces protected
8 the encouragement of small businesses to help provide jobs
9 a very good scheme because it put people first – should be a model for other cities

⊙━ 9

First paragraph: Paragraph E
1 Pakistan's   2 Karachi   3 Islamabad

⊙━ 10

E D A C B F
E This article describes the background to the choice and development of Islamabad as the modern capital of Pakistan. When the new state of Pakistan was founded in 1947, Karachi acted as the capital city. However, it was difficult for Karachi to remain in this role due to a number of drawbacks such as the climate and the state of the existing buildings.
(repeating key word)
D Rather than try to overcome these drawbacks, the government decided to create a new capital city. In 1959, a commission was established to investigate the possible locations of this new city. The advisor appointed to the commission was Dr Doxiadis, a famous architect and city planner.
(repeating key word)
A Dr Doxiadis and his colleagues looked at the various locations. They then produced a report suggesting two possible areas: one just outside Karachi and the other to the north of Rawalpindi. Both locations had advantages as well as disadvantages. Which site was it to be?
(question)
C The choice between these two options was made after consideration of many factors, such as transportation, the availability of water, economic factors, and factors of national interest. Finally, the site north of Rawalpindi was chosen and on the 24th February 1960, the new capital was given the name of 'Islamabad' and a master plan was drawn up. This master plan divided the area into three different sections: Islamabad itself, neighbouring Rawalpindi, and the national park.
(continuing the topic)
B Each of these three sections had a different role. Islamabad would act as the nation's capital and would serve its administrative and cultural needs, whereas Rawalpindi would remain the regional centre with industry and commerce. The third piece of the plan, the national park, was planned to provide space for education, recreation, and agriculture.
F Today Islamabad is a thriving city of about one million people. It offers a healthy climate, a pollution-free atmosphere, plenty of water, and many green spaces. It has wide, tree-lined streets, elegant public buildings, and well-organized bazaars and shopping centres. The new capital is a superb example of good urban planning.

⊙━ 11

1 The country of Pakistan was created in 1947.
2 Dr Doxiadis was made an advisor to the commission.
3 The initial report described two places which could be used for the new capital.
4 The master plan split the new area into three sections.
5 Rawalpindi was to maintain its role as the regional centre.
6 The capital is still doing well.

RESEARCH Finding information p23

AIMS

The aim of this section is to help students find information in reference books and on the Internet more efficiently by using different words to search by, and by choosing the most appropriate and reliable search engines.

LEAD IN

- Write the word *jobs* on the board. Ask:
  – *Can you give me a synonym for 'jobs'?* (employment/work/professions/careers/posts/positions)
- You may wish to explain the idea of 'near synonyms' (words that have the same general meaning but may not be completely interchangeable depending on the context).

PROCEDURE

1 Tell students to read the **Study Skill** and the instructions. Students complete the tasks individually. Put students in pairs to compare their answers. **⊶ 1**

2 Students read the instructions and complete the task individually. Write the table on the board and ask some students to write in their answers. The rest of the class compare their answers. **⊶ 2**

3 Tell students to read the **Study Skill**. You may wish to explain to students that a *subject directory* is a list of sources usually provided by universities on an academic subject. Students would have to scan the list and choose the sources that they thought would be useful.

Students read the instructions and complete the task individually. Put students in pairs to compare their answers. Ask some students to tell the class their ideas. There may be more than one possible answer, so if students have different ideas, ask them to explain their answers to the class. **⊶ 3**

4 Tell students to read the **Study Skill**. Some time should be spent on clarifying the symbols used. Students read the instructions and work in pairs to complete the task. Ask some students to write their answers on the board. The rest of the class compare their answers. **⊶ 4**

BACKGROUND INFORMATION

You may wish to remind students that some information from websites is not reliable, and that it is advisable to check the information on two or more sites.

Point out to students that the purpose of a site may indicate its reliability.

Suggest that students ask themselves:

Who is this website for? (professionals, students, anyone)

Who produced this website? Look at the end of the URL (address of a WORLD WIDE WEB page). This will tell you the type of source it is, e.g. *.com* is a commercial company or individual, *.gov* is a site produced by a government agency, etc.

Why has this site been created? (to advertise, educate, make money, etc.)

Is this site 'open' (anyone can add, delete, or edit the content) *or 'closed'* (visitors to the site cannot alter it)?

Closed sites are likely to be more reliable than sites which are open.

EXTENSION ACTIVITY

Tell students to visit the following sites and find out if they are 'open' or 'closed' sites.

http://en.wikipedia.org/wiki/Qin_Dynasty (open)

http://www.britannica.com/ebc/article-9376232 (closed)

RESEARCH Answer key p23

⊶ 1

2f 3d 4b 5e 6h 7a 8c

⊶ 2

infrastructure: bridges, roads, sanitation
scientists: biologist, physicist, chemist
public buildings: hospital, museum, post office
education: diploma, seminar, curriculum

⊶ 3

1 a search engine, e.g. Google
2 a search engine / a site where you can type a direct question, e.g. http://uk.ask.com
3 a subject directory
4 Google or online encyclopaedia
5 Google or other search engine; or a subject directory and then scan for relevant sources

⊶ 4

Possible answers

2 Canberra +design / design +Canberra
3 "early cities" +Asia
4 history +Istanbul / Istanbul +history
5 "famous architects" -America

WRITING   An international trade fair   pp24–25

AIMS

The aim of this section is to focus students' attention on the importance of selecting relevant information and prioritizing it correctly. Students will also practise the skill of brainstorming for ideas, and will write a persuasive article.

LEAD IN

- Ask: *What is a trade fair? Has anyone been to a trade fair?*
  If yes, ask:
  – *Where was it?* – *What area(s) of trade/industry were represented?*
  – *What did you think of it?*

PROCEDURE

1 Students read the instructions and work in pairs or small groups to complete the task. Copy the table onto the board. Ask some students to complete the table. The rest of the class compares answers. **⊶ 1**

2 Students read the instructions and complete the task. They discuss the answers in pairs. Accept different answers if students can justify and explain their decision. Tell students to read the **Study Skill**. **⊶ 2**

3 Students read the instructions and work individually to complete the task. Put students in pairs or small groups to compare their answers. Ask some students to explain their choices to the class. Almost any two are acceptable as the most important, as long as students can justify them. Tell students to read the **Study Skill**. **⊶ 3**

4 Students read the instructions. Students in pairs or small groups put the information from each category in the order of importance. Ask some groups to tell the class the order they put the information in, and to explain why. **⊶ 4**

5 Students read the instructions. Tell students to read the example paragraph. Ask:
– *What linking words are used?* (because, when, Furthermore)
Students work individually to write a paragraph about
– location   – facilities   – weather   – trade and industry
This exercise could be set for homework. **⊶ 5**

6 Students read the instructions. Ask:
– *What does the introduction tell us?* (the purpose of the article and the order the information will be presented in)
Students may change the order of the topics in the introduction to match the order of importance they decided on in exercise 4. Tell students to go back to the **Study Skill** on p20 to remind themselves how to make links between one paragraph and another. **⊶ 6**

Writing a persuasive article   p25

7 Tell students to read the **Study Skill**. Emphasize that in order to brainstorm well, it is important not to be critical of ideas and reject them. Every suggestion or idea should be noted down at this stage.

Students read the instructions and work in pairs to complete the task. Write the headings on the board and ask some students to come up and write down their ideas. Ask the rest of the class to add other ideas to each category. Do not discuss which are important and which are not at this stage. **⊶ 7**

8 Students read the instructions. Students work in pairs and decide which event they wish to hold. Ask some students to explain the reasons for their choice.

Students continue working in their pairs and decide which information from the table in exercise 7 is relevant to the type of event they wish to hold. You may wish to take one event as an example and go through the information in the table from exercise 7 to discuss which information is relevant, and which is not.

Tell students to choose 2 or 3 pieces of information from each category. **⊶ 8**

9 Students read the instructions and work individually to complete the task.

Remind students to prioritize the information they chose in exercise 8, and to use words and phrases to link their ideas from sentence to sentence, and from paragraph to paragraph. The writing could be set as homework.

WRITING   Answer key   pp24–25

⊶ 1

transportation
1   an international airport 20km away
2   a good network of roads to other parts of the country
11   an excellent public transport system
15   many private cars

location
5   only 30 minutes away from capital city
8   a mountain range about 5km away
13   only 10km from two international borders
19   on the coast

facilities
3   several top-quality restaurants
7   a 20-hectare site ready for re-development
9   hotel accommodation for 20,000 visitors
20   a university

weather
4   doesn't usually rain in the summer
6   average summer temperature is 24° C
14   a very low level of air pollution because of coastal winds
16   snows heavily in the winter

trade and industry
10   the centre for gold marketing and jewellery making
12   a world famous computer manufacturer based in the city
17   famous for its boat-building industry
18   lots of shops

⊶ 2

Possible answers

transportation – many private cars (visitors to fair won't need these)
location – mountain range 5km away (doesn't concern visitors whereas the rest show how accessible Urbania is)
facilities – a university (irrelevant to trade fair)
weather – snows heavily in winter (fair to be held in summer)
trade and industry – lots of shops (trade fairs are about large scale sales of products and means of production and expertise, not about shopping)

⊶ 3

Possible answers

transportation (getting visitors to the trade fair is essential)
location (same reason as transportation – visitors need to know where Urbania is)

⊶ 4

Possible answers
location
(1)   only 30 minutes away from capital city
(2)   only 10km from two international borders
(3)   on the coast

facilities
(1)   a 20-hectare site ready for re-development
(2)   hotel accommodation for 20,000 visitors
(3)   several top-quality restaurants

weather
(1)   average summer temperature is 24° C
(2)   doesn't usually rain in summer
(3)   a very low level of air pollution because of coastal winds

trade and industry
(1)   a world famous computer manufacturer based in the city
(2)   the centre for gold marketing and jewellery making
(3)   famous for its boat-building industry

⊶ 5   Students' own answers.

⊶ 6   Students' own answers.

⊶ 7   Students' own answers.

⊶ 8   Students' own answers.

⊶ 9   Students' own answers.

4 Water, food, and energy

READING SKILLS Finding information from more than one source • Identifying language for rephrasing and giving examples
LANGUAGE FOR WRITING Introductions and conclusions • Rephrasing and giving examples
WRITING SKILLS Introductions • Developing a thesis statement • Conclusions • Checking your writing (3)
            Writing to describe and explain
VOCABULARY DEVELOPMENT Compound nouns • Compound adjectives

READING Water, water, everywhere pp28–29

AIMS

The aim of this section is to give students practice in finding and comparing information from more than one source, and in recognizing language for rephrasing, explaining, and giving examples.

LEAD IN

- If you think your students would be interested in the poem, write the verse in the Background Information box on the board. Explain that it is taken from a poem. Ask:
  - *The writer is surrounded by water. Where do you think he is?* (on a boat/ship at sea)
  - *What could the 'boards' be?* (the deck of the boat)
  - *If there is water everywhere, why can't he drink it?* (because it's sea water/salt water)

BACKGROUND INFORMATION

The title for this section comes from a verse in the poem 'The Rime of the Ancient Mariner' by Samuel Coleridge.

Water, water, every where,

And all the boards did shrink;

Water, water, every where,

Nor any drop to drink.

- If you don't think they would be interested in the poem, focus students' attention on the page. Ask students to identify the skill READING, and the topic (*Water, water everywhere*). Ask:
  - *What do you understand by the title?*
  - *Is water everywhere?* (no!)
  - *Where is there a lot of water?* (in the seas and oceans)
  - *Is there enough water in your country?*

PROCEDURE

1 Students read the instructions and discuss the statements in pairs or small groups. Ask some students to give the class their ideas. **⊙⃫ 1**

2 Students read the instructions. Ask for their ideas. **⊙⃫ 2**

3 Students read the instruction and complete the task. Get students to work in pairs to compare answers. **⊙⃫ 3**

4 Students read the **Study Skill** and the instructions. Students read *Text A* and complete the task.

5 Students read the instructions and *Text B* and complete the task.

6 Students read the instructions and complete the task individually. Students compare their answers with a partner. **⊙⃫ 6**

READING Answer key pp28–30

⊙⃫ 1

Students' own answers.

⊙⃫ 2

The articles come from a magazine, and they are for a general reader.

⊙⃫ 3

70% The surface of the Earth which is water.
98% The percentage of this water which is salt water.
1972 The date the United Arab Emirates installed the first desalination plants according to *Text A*.
300 billion (litres) The amount of desalinated water produced annually by one plant in Saudi Arabia.
25% Percentage of the world's desalinated water produced by Saudi Arabia / The percentage of the world's population who live within 25 kilometres of the sea.
32,000 (kilometres) The length of the coastline in China.
2.7 billion (litres) The amount of fresh water which will be required daily in the UAE in 2015.
150 (litres) The average daily consumption of water per person.

⊙⃫ 4

1   A process to convert salt water to fresh water *(Text A)*
2   salt and contaminants *(Text A)*
3   heating process and filtration methods *(Text A)*
4   UAE, Saudi Arabia, China *(Text A)*
5   1970s *(Text A)*   1958 *(Text B)*
6   by combining the plant with a power station *(Text B)*
7   1972 *(Text A)*   1960 *(Text B)*
8   leakages and loss of water, increase in water consumption *(Text B)*
9   limit consumption, repair pipes *(Text B)*
10 new technology to lower costs of desalination *(Text A)* water companies will have to work efficiently and public will learn water is a precious resource *(Text B)*

Food chains p30

LEAD IN

- Ask:
  - *Where does our food come from?* (supermarkets, shops, plants and animals, etc.)
  - *What do we depend on for our food?* (other living things)

PROCEDURE

7 Students look at the title (*Food chains*), and read the instructions. Students work in pairs or small groups to answer the questions. Elicit students' answers and write them on the board. Do not correct at this stage.

8 Students read the instructions and complete the task. Students compare the answers with those on the board. ⌐ 8

9 Students read the instructions and work in pairs or small groups to complete the task. Remind students to mark the stress, the part of speech, and any other information which is useful. ⌐ 9

10 Students read the instructions and complete the task individually. Students compare their answers with a partner. ⌐ 10

11 Tell students to read the **Study Skill**. Students complete the task in pairs or small groups. There are two examples with *such as*. ⌐ 11

12 Students read the instructions and complete the task individually. ⌐ 12

⌐ 8

1 c 2 a 3 b

⌐ 9

decomposers (n) = living things that break down or destroy dead animals using natural chemical processes
photosynthesis (n)= the process by which green plants make food using light and carbon dioxide
herbivores (n) = animals which only eat grass and plants
omnivores (n) = animals which eat everything, plants and other animals/meat
carnivores (n) = animals which eat only meat

⌐ 10

1 photosynthesis 2 herbivores 3 carnivores 4 omnivores
5 decomposers

⌐ 11

Green plants <u>are an example of</u> a producer.
They use photosynthesis, <u>that is</u>, the process of …
These organic compounds are found in various parts of the plant <u>such as</u> the leaves …
<u>Examples of this are</u> sheep eating grass, …
<u>For instance</u>, when humans eat vegetables, they are primary consumers.
<u>In other words</u>, they are directly eating a product of photosynthesis.
When the final consumer dies, its body is broken down into simple molecules by decomposers <u>such as</u> bacteria and fungi, …

⌐ 12

1 producers, consumers, and decomposers
2 producers: plants
  consumers: animals and humans
  decomposers: bacteria and fungi
3 It depends what it eats. If it eats vegetables (plants), it is consuming the direct product of photosynthesis, and, therefore, is a primary consumer. If it eats meat, it is a secondary consumer.
4 They are broken down (decomposed) into simple molecules which go back into the soil to be used by plants.

LANGUAGE FOR WRITING p31
Introductions and conclusions

AIMS
The aim of this section is help students to recognize and use fixed phrases and linking words that are commonly used in academic writing.

PROCEDURE

1 Students read the instructions and complete the task. Students compare their answers with a partner. Write the sentences on the board and ask some students to underline the phrases. The rest of the class compares answers. **⊙ 1**

2 Students read the instructions and complete the task individually. Students compare their answers with a partner. **⊙ 2**

3 Students read the instructions and complete the task individually. Students compare their answers with a partner. Write the table on the board. Ask some students to come up and complete it. **⊙ 3**

Rephrasing and giving examples p31

4 Students read the instructions and complete the task individually. Students compare their answers with a partner. **⊙ 4**

5 Students read the instructions and complete the task individually. Ask some students to read out their sentences. The rest of the class listens and compares their answers. **⊙ 5**

6 Students read the instructions and complete the task in pairs or small groups. Ask some pairs or groups to read out their answers. **⊙ 6**

ADDITIONAL PHOTOCOPIABLE ACTIVITY

Writing 4 Writing introductions and conclusions

LANGUAGE FOR WRITING Answer key p31

⊙ 1

1 This essay will describe the three types of organisms which form food chains and explain how each organism acts as a food source for the next one in the chain.

2 To summarize, a food chain shows that every organism is dependent on another for its source of energy and in turn, acts as a food source for the next organism in the chain.

⊙ 2

1 This report will outline the problems caused by water shortages.

2 In conclusion, there are two main solutions to this problem.

3 In brief, it is essential to reduce the pollution of the oceans.

4 Two aspects of energy conservation will be discussed in this article.

5 As this report has shown, new developments in technology are essential.

6 In this paper the problems will be examined in detail and some solutions will be proposed.

⊙ 3

Introductions	Summarizing and concluding
This essay will describe ...	To summarize, ...
This report will outline ...	In conclusion, ...
... will be discussed ...	In brief, ...
In this paper ... will be examined ...	As this report has shown, ...

⊙ 4

Consumers are classified depending on their place in the chain. For instance, when humans eat vegetables, they are primary consumers. In other words, they are directly eating a product of photosynthesis. When they eat meat, they are secondary consumers.

⊙ 5

1 c Photosynthesis, that is the process by which plants make food, requires sunlight.

2 b Primary consumers, for example cows, feed on plants.

3 a A hydro-electric plant, in other words a power station using water to make electricity, will be built on the coast.

4 d Microorganisms, such as bacteria and fungi, are the final step in the food chain.

⊙ 6

Possible answers

1 pasta/potatoes/rice
2 the inability to sleep
3 process by which living things produce energy from food
4 crocodiles/snakes

WRITING   Sources of energy   pp32–33

AIMS
The aim of this section is to give students practice in writing introductions (including thesis statements) and conclusions.

LEAD IN
- Write *Sources of energy* on the board. Elicit different sources (coal, oil, the sun, food, etc). Ask:
  - *What energy problems does the world face?*
  - *Why?*

PROCEDURE

1 Tell students to read the **Study Skill**. Students read the instructions and complete the task individually. Students compare their answers with a partner. 🔑 **1**

2 Students read the instructions and complete the task individually. Students compare their answers with a partner. 🔑 **2**

3 Students read the instructions and complete the task individually. Students compare their answers with a partner. Ask students what is wrong with the other possible answers (too detailed or too vague). 🔑 **3**

4 Tell students to read the **Study Skill**. Students read the instructions and complete the task individually. Students compare their answers with a partner. Ask some students to read their answers aloud. Choose two or three and write them on the board. Ask the class to vote on which one is best. If the students disagree, ask them to explain why. 🔑 **4**

5 Students read the instructions and discuss their answers with a partner. Elicit the answers from the students. Tell students to read the **Study Skill**. 🔑 **5**

6 Students read the instructions and complete the task individually. Students compare their answers with a partner. 🔑 **6**

Writing to describe and explain   p33

7 Students read the instructions and complete the task with a partner. 🔑 **7**

8 Students read the instructions. Ask students to recall what must come in the different paragraphs (direct them to the **Study Skill** on p24). Students do the task with a partner.

9 Students read the instructions and do the task individually. Students compare their answers with a partner (direct students to the **Study Skill** on p32).

10 Students read the instructions and write their essay.

11 Tell students to read the **Study Skill** and complete the task. You can encourage students to read each other's essays and comment on the content and organization of each paragraph. See 'Writing a comparing and contrasting essay' on p9 of the Teacher's Guide for 'peer correction'.

EXTENSION ACTIVITY
When students have finished writing, tell them to check their work for errors of punctuation (e.g. full stops, commas with linking words, capital letters, and spelling). Students may refer to the **Study Skill** on p11. Put students into pairs to check each other's work for mistakes that were missed.

WRITING   Answer key   pp32–33

🔑 **1**

A food chain shows the relationship between organisms which feed on each other. <u>This essay will describe the three types of organisms which form food chains, and explain how each organism acts as a food source for the next one in the chain.</u>

🔑 **2**

a 2   b 3   c 1

🔑 **3**

1 c   2 b

🔑 **4**

Model answer
Solar power is energy from the sun which is used for heating, cooking, and providing light. This essay will describe the advantages and disadvantages of this alternative source of energy.

🔑 **5**

It includes a concluding remark (see *Language for Writing*, page 31). It has a summary of the main points. It includes the writer's opinion (hopes) for the future.

🔑 **6**

Model answer
In conclusion, solar power is an important source of energy, especially in sunny countries. Although there are disadvantages, these are outnumbered by the advantages. It is hoped that solar power will be further developed in the future.

🔑 **7**

Possible answers
Energy conservation: oil crisis, shortage of fossil fuels, pollution, global warming
Reduce pollution: use public transport more, switch off appliances when not in use, turn down heating/air conditioning, more recycling

🔑 **8**

Students' own answers.

🔑 **9**

Students' own answers.

🔑 **10**

Students' own answers.

VOCABULARY DEVELOPMENT
Compound nouns and adjectives p34

AIMS
The aims of this section are to make students aware that vocabulary items often consist of more than one word, and to help them recognize this compound vocabulary.

LEAD IN
- Dictate a few compound nouns to the students, e.g. *post office, armchair, notebook, tablecloth*. Ask:
  – *What do you notice about these words?* (they are formed from two nouns)

PROCEDURE
1 Tell students to read the **Study Skill**. Students read the instructions and complete the task individually. Students compare answers with a partner. Elicit the answers. **⊶ 1**

2 Students read the instructions and complete the task individually. Remind students that compound words can be written in different ways, that is, as one word, or two words with or without a hyphen. Encourage them to use a dictionary to check. Students compare their answers with a partner. Elicit the answers. **⊶ 2**

3 Students read the instructions and complete the task in pairs or small groups. Elicit the answers. **⊶ 3**

4 Tell students to read the **Study Skill**. Ask:
  – *What is a present participle?* (-ing form)
  – What is a past participle? (the third form of the verb, e.g. know, knew, **known**).

Students read the instructions. Tell students to look at the example answer. Elicit how the compound adjective was formed. Students complete the task individually and compare their answers with a partner. Elicit the answers. Remind students that these adjectives are hyphenated. **⊶ 4**

BACKGROUND INFORMATION
Compound adjectives are usually hyphenated. However, if they come after the noun they modify, they are usually not hyphenated. For example:
The densely-populated inner city areas are being redeveloped.
The inner city areas are densely populated and are being redeveloped.

EXTENSION ACTIVITY
Ask students to find other compound nouns and adjectives from their field of study and present them to the class.

⊶ 1

1 There are several tips for succeeding in your studies. Keep good vocabulary records in your <u>notebook</u>. Do your <u>homework</u> regularly. Make sure that your <u>handwriting</u> is easy to read.
2 The Antarctic <u>food chain</u> is a simple example. Plankton, that is, tiny plants that live in <u>sea water</u>, are the producers in this chain. Using <u>carbon dioxide</u> and <u>sunlight</u>, they produce food through photosynthesis and are fed on by krill. Krill are small animals, the primary consumers in this chain. They, in turn, are eaten by whales. The whales are the secondary consumers and the next step in the chain.
3 Music has long been used to treat patients suffering from many different conditions. It has been shown that patients suffering from <u>backache</u> recovered more quickly if they listened to music every morning. A fast <u>heartbeat</u> can also be slowed down by music.

⊶ 2

1 b guidelines
2 d fossil fuels
3 e lab coat
4 a skyscrapers
5 f mineral water
6 c briefcase

⊶ 3

1 guidelines
2 lab coat
3 Skyscrapers
4 fossil fuels
5 mineral water
6 briefcase

⊶ 4

2 man-made
3 fast-growing
4 well-written
5 frequently-occurring
6 home-grown
7 well-built
8 life-threatening
9 rapidly-increasing
10 boat-building

REVIEW p35

AIMS

The aims of this section are to give students further practice in the skills learnt in this unit, and to give them the opportunity to review the work they have done. A further aim is to encourage students to apply what they have learnt to their academic studies in English.

PROCEDURE

1 Students read the instructions. Students work individually and compare their answers with a partner. Elicit one or two answers and write them on the board. Ask which one they prefer and why. **⚷ 1**

2 Students read the instructions. Ask the students to recall the main contents of a conclusion. Students complete the task individually and compare their answers with a partner. **⚷ 2**

3 Students read the instructions. Explain that more than one answer is possible. Students do the task in pairs or small groups. **⚷ 3**

4 Students read the instructions and complete the task. **⚷ 4**

5 Students read the instructions. Elicit how compound adjectives are formed. Students complete the task. **⚷ 5**

EXTENSION ACTIVITY

Ask the students to list the skills they have learnt and practised in this unit. For example:

– comparing information from more than one source
– how to rephrase difficult or new words, and how to give examples
– how to write introductions including a thesis statement, and how to write conclusions

Put students into small groups to discuss how they could apply these skills to their academic studies.

This activity could be set as homework.

REVIEW Answer key p35

⚷ 1

Model answers

1 This essay will explain the phenomenon of global warming and describe several possible causes of it.
2 Pollution is a major problem in many countries in the world today. The importance of reducing pollution will be discussed in this essay.
3 A well-balanced diet is important to keep healthy. This essay will outline the consequences of a poor diet on our health.

⚷ 2

Model answer

In conclusion, the wind is a free source of energy which is particularly useful in windy countries. As this essay has shown, it is inexpensive to produce and it is already in use in some countries.

⚷ 3

1 that is/in other words
2 such as
3 such as /for example
4 that is/in other words

⚷ 4

1 notebooks
2 well-organized
3 lunchtime
4 English-speaking
5 comprehensive school
6 fossil fuel
7 stomach-ache
8 rainwater
9 newspaper

⚷ 5

1 diet-related   2 water-saving   3 well-managed
4 decision-making   5 poorly-maintained

5 Free trade and fair trade

READING SKILLS Distinguishing between facts, speculation, and reported opinions • Identifying a point of view
LANGUAGE FOR WRITING Expressing certainty, uncertainty, and caution
WRITING SKILLS Supporting a point of view • Presenting arguments (1) and (2) • Writing an opinion essay
VOCABULARY DEVELOPMENT Using a dictionary (3)

READING Globalization pp36–37

AIMS

The aim of this section is to improve students' ability to assess a text by distinguishing what is expressed as fact, speculation, or an opinion, and then to identify a point of view.

LEAD IN

- Tell students to read the unit heading *Free trade and fair trade*. Ask:
  – *What do you think the difference is between 'free trade' and 'fair trade'?*
- Put students' ideas on the board. Focus students' attention on the page. Ask students to identify the skill READING, and the topic (*Globalization*).

PROCEDURE

1 Students read the instructions and discuss the answers in pairs. Ask some students to tell the class their ideas. **⚬┑ 1**

2 Students read the instructions and the title of the article, and then decide if they think globalization is a good thing or a bad thing. You may wish to have a show of hands in the class to see how many students think it is good, and how many think it is bad. Ask some students to tell the class why they think it is either good or bad.

3 Students read the instructions and complete the task individually. Set a time limit of 30 seconds. Elicit the answers from the class. **⚬┑ 3**

4 Students read the instructions and complete the task individually. Students compare their answers in pairs. Ask some pairs to tell the rest of the class their answers. **⚬┑ 4**

5 Students read the **Study Skill** and the instructions. Students complete the task working individually, and then compare their answers in pairs. You may wish to set a time limit for this activity (three minutes) to encourage students to scan the article rather than read it intensively. **⚬┑ 5**

6 Students read the instructions and complete the task individually. Students compare answers in small groups.

  You may wish to get students to time this reading, using the method described in the extension activity on p7 of the Teacher's Guide.

  Go through the answers with the whole class. **⚬┑ 6** p31

7 Students read the instructions. Students complete the task and compare answers in pairs. Write the words on the board and ask some students to come up and write in the missing words. **⚬┑ 7** p31

8 Students read the instructions and complete the task individually. Ask some students to read out their sentences. The rest of the class compare their answers. **⚬┑ 8** p31

BACKGROUND INFORMATION

The GDP (gross domestic product) is the total value of all goods and services produced by a country in one year.

The GNP (gross national product) is the total value of all goods and services produced by a country in one year, including the total income from foreign countries.

READING Answer key pp36–38

⚬┑ 1 Students' own answers.

⚬┑ 2 Students' own answers.

⚬┑ 3

1 Four (or five if the concluding paragraph is considered a separate section)
2 Three
3 Three
4 The writer isn't clearly either for or against globalization; it is a balanced article but the writer believes there needs to be a fairer balance between free and fair trade.

⚬┑ 4

For globalization:
Everyone in a country gets more money from international trade.
Business develops between two countries.
Free trade countries develop expertise in an industry and get a bigger market.
Against globalization:
Only a minority get more money, most people don't.
Farmers are forced to sell their produce at low prices and buy manufactured goods at high prices.
Developing an expertise in one or two industries forces countries to import all other goods.

⚬┑ 5

Globalization is defined in many ways. One simple definition is that it is the rapid increase in international free trade, investment, and technological exchange. **It is argued** that this international trade … some people **believe** that this growth has only benefitted certain countries, and that others have suffered as a result. Which argument is correct?
Improved income?
An argument in favour of globalization is that the benefits of …
It would appear that countries which open their doors to world trade tend to become wealthier.
However, these sorts of figures ⟨might⟩ not be giving a true picture …
More imports, more exports
Supporters of free trade **point out** that there is another direct benefit to be gained from an increase in international trade: exports require imports …
Critics **maintain** that, in general, it is poorer countries which produce and export food such as coffee … Furthermore, it is the richer countries which control the price of commodities and therefore, farmers ⟨may⟩ be forced to sell their produce at a low price and to buy manufactured goods at an inflated price.
Industrial development
Finally, globalization often encourages a country to focus on industries which are already successful …
Anti-globalists **claim** that there is a serious flaw in this argument for the specialization of industry. Countries which only focus on one or two main industries are forced to import other goods. These imported goods are frequently over-priced, and these countries, therefore, have a tendency to accumulate huge debts.

This debate will ⟨undoubtedly⟩ continue for some time. However, it would seem that that a better balance between free trade and fair trade is the answer to the problems of globalization.

Is 'fair trade' fair? p38

9 Students read the instructions. Give students 60 seconds maximum to complete the task. Check the answers with the whole class. Tell students to read the **Study Skill**. 🔑 9

10 Students read the instructions and work in pairs to complete the task. Draw the table on the board and ask some students to complete the missing information. The rest of the class compares their answers. 🔑 10

11 Students read the instructions and complete the task individually. Elicit answers from the class. 🔑 11

EXTENSION ACTIVITY

Get students to go through the texts in this unit making a note of any new vocabulary that was not dealt with. Encourage students to be selective about the vocabulary they record. They should only choose words that will be useful to them.

Tell students to record the new vocabulary, using an appropriate method.

🔑 6

1 (S) It is argued that this international trade has been one of the main causes of world economic growth over the past half century.
2 (F) Although there is little doubt that the global economy has grown enormously in the last 50 years,
3 (F) An example of this is China, where per capita income rose from about $1400 in 1980 to over $4000 by 2000.
4 (F) Countries which produce and export coffee import the packaging for it, ...
5 (F) ... a two-way trade which enables commerce to develop in two countries at the same time.
6 (S) ... farmers may be forced to sell their produce at a low price ...
7 (S) ... these countries, therefore, have a tendency to accumulate huge debts.

🔑 7

1 international trade   2 the global economy
3 world trade, world market   4 a substantial increase
5 the vast majority   6 a slight improvement
7 a direct benefit   8 manufactured goods
9 an inflated price   10 a serious flaw

🔑 8

1 A reduction in the cost of flying has led to a **substantial increase** in international tourism.
2 India and China's share of the **global economy / world market** is expected to increase over the next ten years.
3 The experiment had to be repeated because there was a **serious flaw** in the equation.
4 Holiday packages are often sold at an **inflated price** during peak seasons such as school holidays.

🔑 9

Letter A is more negative.
Letter B is more objective.
Letter C is more positive.

🔑 10

Letter A (negative points)
1 *high prices for the goods*
2 profit not passed on to producers
Letter B (positive points)
1 consumers more aware of how food produced
2 farmers and traders in poor countries benefit
Letter B (negative points)
1 increase in air transport = pollution
2 decrease in food production for own country
Letter C (positive points)
1 improvement for small farmers and producers in developing countries
2 profit goes to people who produced food
3 can get a higher price and bigger profit margin
4 high-quality food for consumers

🔑 11

1 a   2 e   3 d   4 f   5 c   6 b

LANGUAGE FOR WRITING
Expressing certainty and uncertainty p39

AIMS
The aim of this section is help students to recognize and use fixed phrases and linking words that are commonly used in academic writing.

PROCEDURE

1 Students read the instructions and underline the modal verbs. **O⊣ 1**

2 Students read instructions and complete the task individually. Ask three students to write the sentences on the board. The rest of the class check their answers. **O⊣ 2**

Remind students that modal verbs are followed by the base infinitive (the infinitive without *to*)

3 Students read the instructions. Students work individually and then compare answers with a partner. **O⊣ 3**

4 Students read the instructions and complete the sentences. Students compare their answers in pairs or small groups.

Elicit some answers and put these on the board. Where there is a difference of opinion, ask students to explain their point of view. **O⊣ 4**

Expressing caution p39

5 Students read the instructions and identify the verb phrases which express caution or a generalization. **O⊣ 5**

6 Students read the instructions and complete the task individually. Students compare their answers in pairs. Ask a student to read the text aloud. The rest of the class compare their answers. **O⊣ 6**

ADDITIONAL PHOTOCOPIABLE ACTIVITY
Writing 5 Giving reasons and examples

LANGUAGE FOR WRITING Answer key p39

O⊣ 1
1 India <u>could</u> be one of the major economic powers of this century.
2 Small companies <u>might</u> also benefit from the increase in world trade.
3 More globalization <u>may</u> have a negative impact on the environment.

O⊣ 2
1 Buying more fair trade food may lead to an increase in the use of planes.
2 Globalization could have an effect on local culture and traditions.
3 An increase in exports might lead to an increase in the number of jobs.

O⊣ 3

adjective	adverb
certain	certainly
clear	clearly
probable	probably
likely	–
possible	possibly
unlikely	–

O⊣ 4
Possible answers
1 One **possible** result of China's greater economic power is that the Chinese language will be taught in schools all over the world. However, it is **unlikely** that this will happen in the near future.
2 An increased demand for fresh water will **probably** result in the greater use of desalination plants. It is also **likely** that the cost of tap water will go up.
3 It is **clear** that the world's population is increasing. An increasing population will **certainly** lead to an increasing demand for food.

O⊣ 5
there has been a tendency (generalization)
it would seem (caution)

O⊣ 6
1 It would appear   2 believe   3 could/may   4 it is likely
5 may/could

WRITING Examples of fair trade pp40-41

AIMS

The aim of this section is to develop the students' ability to express arguments and to present support for those arguments in an opinion essay.

LEAD IN

- Ask:
  - *What is fair trade?* (a system whereby producers are paid fairly for their produce and are helped to develop their own businesses, and to help their local communities)
- If students cannot remember, tell them to re-read Letter C on p38.

PROCEDURE

1 Students read the instructions and scan the paragraph for the answers. Elicit answers from the class. **⊙━ 1**

Tell students to read the **Study Skill**. Explain that in academic writing, arguments or opinions should always be supported by evidence and examples.

2 Students read the instructions and complete the task individually. Remind students of the importance of a topic sentence (see **Study Skill** on p12). **⊙━ 2**

Consumerism pp40–41

3 Students read the instructions and discuss the title in pairs or small groups. Ask some students to explain to the class what they understand by *consumerism*. **⊙━ 3**

4 Students read the instructions and complete the task individually. Elicit answers from the class. **⊙━ 4**

5 Students read the instructions and brainstorm (see **Study Skill** on p25) the topics in pairs or small groups. **⊙━ 5**

6 Tell students to read the **Study Skill**. Explain that neither method is better than the other. The important thing is to be consistent, that is, use the same method throughout the essay.

Students read the instructions and complete the task. Students discuss their answers in pairs. Elicit the answers from the class. **⊙━ 6**

7 Students read the instructions and complete the task. Put students in small groups to discuss their answers. Elicit the answers from the class. Ask students to justify their answers. **⊙━ 7**

8 Students read the instructions and discuss the answers in pairs. Elicit the answers from the class. Tell students to read the **Study Skill**. **⊙━ 8**

Writing an opinion essay p41

9 Students read the instructions and discuss the best approach in pairs or small groups. You may wish to point out that arguments *for* and *against* are similar for cars, tourism, and clothes, so it would be more sensible to organize ideas by viewpoint, i.e. arguments for in one paragraph, arguments against in another.

Put students into small groups to discuss whether they are for, against, or neutral about globalization. Explain that the essay does not necessarily have to represent their true opinion.

Students put their arguments in order. Remind them that they should put what they believe to be the strongest argument first (or last).

Students write their thesis statement (see **Study Skill** on p32).

You can ask some students to read out their thesis statements to the class.

10 Students write the essay. This could be set for homework. **⊙━ 10**

EXTENSION ACTIVITY

Students should exchange their essays from exercise 10 with a partner. Tell students to look for and mark errors in:
– spelling   – linking words

Tell students to go through the essay again to look at sentence length. Students should highlight any sentences which they think are too long or too short.

WRITING Answer key pp40-41

⊙━ 1

a sentence (1) b sentence (2) c sentences (3) and (4)

⊙━ 2

Model answer

Fair trade is a movement which encourages the development of local communities and, at the same time, helps to reduce damage to the environment. Many producers of fair trade goods use their financial and technical expertise in their own communities. An illustration of this is the coffee co-operative in Mexico which started a public bus service in their village. Fair trade producers are encouraged to use systems which allow the soil to recover naturally without chemicals. For example, a group of producers of organic rice in Thailand use traditional techniques which do not use chemicals or exhaust the soil.

⊙━ 3 Possible answer

The belief that it is good for a society or an individual person to buy and use a large quantity of goods and services.

⊙━ 4

a negative   b positive   c negative   d negative
e positive   f negative   g positive

⊙━ 5

cars:
   (-) more pollution, more illnesses like asthma, more traffic jams, more accidents
   (+) more jobs, more freedom to travel
tourism:
   (-) more pollution from planes, etc., more development of unspoilt areas, more places looking the same
   (+) people find out more about other places, more money in the local and national economies
clothes:
   (-) more people working in poor conditions to produce clothes, more packaging and waste
   (+) more jobs, more choice for consumers

⊙━ 6

A by topic (food, then transport, then tourism, and then clothing)
B by viewpoint (disadvantages then advantages)

⊙━ 7

1 essay B   2 essay B   3 essay A   4 essay A

⊙━ 8

First body paragraph: essay B sentence 2 (The main argument ...), essay A sentence 4 (In the first place ...)
Second body paragraph: essay B sentence 1 (Another strong argument ...), essay A sentence 3 (The second point ...)

⊙━ 10

Students' own answers.

VOCABULARY DEVELOPMENT

Multiple meanings p42

AIMS

The aim of this section is to make students aware that some words have more than one meaning, and that a dictionary can help them to locate the correct definition.

LEAD IN

- Ask:
  - *What information does a dictionary entry give?* (meaning, pronunciation, part of speech, irregular plurals or past forms, example sentences, etc.)

PROCEDURE

1 Tell students to read the **Study Skill**. Emphasize that they should always read the example sentence to make sure they have chosen the correct definition. Students read the instructions and complete the task individually.

Check the answers with the whole class. 🔑 1

2 Students read the instructions and work in pairs to complete the task. Elicit the answers from the class. 🔑 2

3 Students read the instructions and work individually to complete the task. Students compare their answers in pairs. 🔑 3

4 Students read the instructions and complete the task individually. Remind students that the pronunciation of *lead* /led/ for the metal and *lead* /liːd/ for the verb are different.

Check the answers with the whole class. 🔑 4

VOCABULARY DEVELOPMENT Answer key p42

🔑 **1**

2 1(1)   3 1(2)   4 1(5)   5 2(1)   6 1(3)   7 1(4)

🔑 **2**

1 a noun b preposition
2 a noun b verb
3 a adjective b noun
4 a noun b adverb
5 a verb b noun

🔑 **3**

2 b hit
  a work stoppage
3 a not influenced by your own personal feelings
  b aim
4 a a short time
  b after the first
5 a become smaller
  b a written legal agreement

🔑 **4**

1 **Lead is** a heavy metal.
2 Astronomers chart the **movement** of stars and planets.
3 After the heavy rain the **ground** was very muddy.
4 The chairman will **lead** the discussions.
5 Coffee beans are roasted and then **ground** into small particles.
6 The earthquake **claimed** many lives.
7 The fair trade **movement** is growing quickly.
8 The research team **claimed** to have found a new cure for malaria.

REVIEW p43

AIMS

The aims of this section are to give students further practice in the skills learnt in this unit, and to give them the opportunity to review the work they have done. A further aim is to encourage students to apply what they have learnt to their academic studies in English.

PROCEDURE

1 Students read the instructions and complete the task in pairs. Check the answers with the class. **O—1**

2 Students read the instructions and complete the task. Students compare their answers in pairs or small groups. **O—2**

3 Students read the instructions. Remind students that a paragraph requires a topic sentence, and that they should use phrases from *Language for Writing* on p31, to show examples. **O—3**

4 Students read the instructions and discuss the words in pairs. Elicit answers from the class. **O—4**

5 Students read the instructions and complete the task individually. Students compare their answers in pairs. Check the answers with the whole class.

Ask:

– *What helped you decide the part of speech?* **O—5**

6 Students read the instructions and complete the task individually. Check the answers with the whole class. **O—6**

REVIEW Answer key p43

O—1

1 negative
2 arguments in favour: 1 (using fewer chemicals is probably better for the environment)
3 arguments against: 3 (it is not proven scientifically that the food itself is better for the consumer; organic food is much more expensive; the overall benefit to the environment is likely to be insignificant as people will continue to buy ordinary food)

O—2

the main argument: 1
support for the argument: 2, 5
examples: 3, 4

O—3

Model answer

In today's world, good information technology (IT) skills are absolutely essential both for education and for work. Students have to find a great deal of information for their studies. However, it is not always easy for students to find the most recent books or journals and this is an example of why being able to use IT is so important. Good IT skills are also required in the workplace. An example of this is the retail trade, where most goods are now electronically coded and controlled using computer technology.

O—4

1 verb (past simple)   2 adjective   3 noun
4 verb (present simple)   5 adjective

O—5

1 noun (preceded by the article a)
2 verb (after *will*, and also there is a subject (*examiner*) and object (*papers*) but no main verb)
3 noun (preceded by the definite article)
4 noun (object of the verb *took*)
5 adjective (in front of a noun)

O—6

1 margin   2 correct   3 rose   4 charge   5 remote

READING SKILLS Dealing with longer texts (1) and (2)
LANGUAGE FOR WRITING Indicating reason or result • Adding information
WRITING SKILLS Checking your writing (4) • Writing an evaluation essay
VOCABULARY DEVELOPMENT Collocations (2)

READING The Terracotta Army pp44–46

AIMS
The aim of this section is to help students develop techniques for dealing with longer texts more effectively.

LEAD IN
- Focus students' attention on the page. Ask students to identify the skill READING, and the topic of the unit (*Conserving the past*).
- Ask:
  - *What does 'conserving the past' mean?* (protecting ancient sites and monuments, repairing and maintaining ancient artefacts)
  - *Who is responsible for doing this?* (Ministry of Culture/Education, museums, archaeologists)

PROCEDURE
1 Students read the instructions. Students discuss their answers in pairs. Elicit students' ideas and write them on the board. Ask:
  - *Who has been to any of these places?*

  Ask students who have visited the places to give a brief description to the rest of the class. **⊶ 1**

2 Students read the instructions and complete the task individually. Set a time limit of 30 seconds. Students compare their answers in pairs. Students then read the **Study Skill. ⊶ 2**

3 Students read the instructions and complete the task. Elicit answers from the class. Ask students to explain their answers. **⊶ 3**

4 Students read the instructions and complete the task individually. Students compare their questions with a partner. Elicit the questions from the class and write them on the board. **⊶ 4**

5 Students read the instructions and complete the task. Set a time limit of 60 seconds to encourage students to skim the text rather than read it intensively. **⊶ 5**

6 Students read the instructions. Set a time limit of two minutes. Tell students to use the information from exercises 4 and 5 to find the answers to the questions as quickly as possible. You could make this a class *race* by asking: *Who can find the answers the quickest?* **⊶ 6**

READING Answer key pp44–46

⊶ 1
Students' own answers.

⊶ 2
1 Ancient China's Terracotta Army
2 5
3 figure 1: terracotta figures
   figure 2: a soldier
   figure 3: a horse and chariot with charioteer
   figure 4: renovation/mending
   figure 5: someone visiting the Terracotta Army

⊶ 3
1 Emperor   2 archer   3 terracotta   4 Chinese   5 chariot

⊶ 4
Possible answers
2 Where was the army found?
3 When was the army built?
4 Who built the army?
5 How many terracotta/clay figures were found/did they find?
6 How many people visit the site?

⊶ 5
1 Paragraph A
2 Paragraph A
3 Paragraph B
4 Paragraph B
5 Paragraph A
6 Paragraph H

⊶ 6
1 in 1974
2 in Qin province, China
3 at the beginning of the 3rd century BCE
4 the Emperor Qin Shi Huang
5 over 8,000
6 nearly two million a year

7 Students read the instructions and complete the task individually. 🔑 7

8 Students read the instructions and complete the task. Encourage students to use a consistent method to write out their notes. 🔑 8

9 Students read the instructions and complete the task. Remind students that thinking about what they have read is an essential part of the academic reading process. 🔑 9

10 Students read the instructions and complete the task. Students then read the **Study Skill**. Emphasize the importance of checking that they have noted the information correctly. 🔑 10

11 Students read the instructions and complete the task. Students then compare their choice of words and phrases in pairs and explain the vocabulary where they can. Remind students of the importance of recording vocabulary appropriately (see **Study Skill** on p18). 🔑 11

EXTENSION ACTIVITY

Tell students to choose a longer text (600–1000 words) from their own field of study. Students should use the SQ3R system to:
– read the text
– highlight the important information
– make notes
Students could present their notes to the rest of the class as a brief class talk.

🔑 7

1 Emperor Qin's achievements:
… <u>became the first emperor of a united China</u>. One of his greatest achievements <u>was the building of the first Great Wall of China</u> to protect China from its enemies. Not all of his achievements were military, however, as he <u>also introduced a common form of writing</u> throughout the country. Nevertheless, outside China he is most famous for his <u>terracotta army</u>.

2 Ancient Chinese belief about the 'afterlife':
At that time the ancient Chinese <u>believed that their 'afterlife' was very similar to their life on earth</u>. Consequently, when they died and were buried, <u>objects which would be useful to them in the next life were buried with them</u>.

3 The way the Chinese craftsmen worked:
<u>In ancient China, however, they used a completely different method. A huge production line was established</u> to make the tens of thousands of individual human and animal statues which Emperor Qin demanded. <u>All the different parts of the body such as legs, arms, and heads were made separately and then assembled</u>. The same process was also used for other pieces such as ears, beards and armour. When the <u>whole figure was completed, it was baked in a kiln, or oven</u>.

4 How the statues got damaged:
It is believed that <u>an invading army robbed the emperor's tomb and then set fire to it. The roofs of the buildings collapsed and fell onto the soldiers and horses</u>.

5 Preserving the statues:
Skilled workers <u>search methodically through hundreds of thousands of</u> fragments to find the right piece to complete each figure. They are lucky if they find one matching piece a day. Because of this, <u>each statue takes several months to be repaired</u>. Furthermore, when the first statues were exposed to the air for the first time in over two thousand years, <u>the paint on them started peeling off or turning black</u>. After extensive research to try and find ways to prevent this problem, <u>scientists now use a chemical solution to protect the paintwork</u>.

🔑 8

1 Emperor Qin's achievements
  1.1 first emperor united China
  1.2 built Great Wall of China
  1.3 introduced common form of writing
  1.4 Terracotta Army
2 Ancient Chinese beliefs about the 'afterlife'
  2.1 believed life was similar after death
  2.2 took objects they would need
3 The way ancient Chinese craftsmen worked
  3.1 huge production line
  3.2 different parts made separately then put together
  3.3 whole figure baked in oven
4 How the statues got damaged
  4.1 invading army robbed the tomb
  4.2 fire destroyed building
  4.3 building collapsed onto statues
5 Preserving the statues
  5.1 search for matching pieces
  5.2 several months to repair each statue
  5.3 chemical solution to stop paint peeling off/going black

🔑 9, 10, 11

Students' own answers.

LANGUAGE FOR WRITING

Indicating reason or result p47

AIMS
The aim of this section is help students to recognize and use fixed phrases and linking words that are commonly used in academic writing.

1 Students read the instructions and work in pairs or small groups to discuss the question. Elicit the answers from the class. **⊙ 1**

2 Students read the instructions and complete the task. Draw the table on the board and ask some students to add the words in the correct place. (Answers after exercise 3) You may wish to point out to students that *so* and *so that* can be easily confused. *So* indicates result and *so that* indicates reason.

3 Students read the instructions and work in pairs to complete the task. Ask some students to add the words and phrases to the table on the board. The rest of the class compare their answers. **⊙ 2 & 3**

4 Students read the **Rules**. Draw their attention to the structure that follows the words and phrases showing reason or result. Students read the instructions and complete the task. Students compare their sentences in pairs. Ask some students to write their sentences on the board. The rest of the class compares their answers. **⊙ 4**

ADDITIONAL PHOTOCOPIABLE ACTIVITY
Writing 6 Indicating reason and result

Adding information p48

PROCEDURE

5 Students read the instructions and work individually. Students compare answers in pairs. **⊙ 5**

6 Students read instructions and complete the task. Elicit the answers from the class. Draw students' attention to the use of a comma after:

In addition,

Furthermore,

What is more,

Moreover,

Note that *as well as* is followed by a noun or gerund. **⊙ 6**

7 Students read the instructions and complete the task individually. Put students in pairs to compare how they have combined the sentences. Remind students about the correct use of commas. Ask some students to write the sentences on the board. The rest of the class compare answers. **⊙ 7**

LANGUAGE FOR WRITING Answer key pp47–48

⊙ 1

1 *Consequently* = result   2 *so that* = reason
3 *As a result* = result

⊙ 2 & 3

Showing reason:	Showing result:
so that	Consequently,
because of (1)	As a result,
in order to (2)	resulted in (3)
since (4)	so (5)
as (6)	Therefore, (7)

⊙ 4

1 c: Large numbers of people from all over the world visit Petra, in Jordan, **because of** its beauty.
2 a: Children are encouraged to visit museums **because** it is important for them to learn about the history of their country.
3 e: Historians are often required to learn languages such as Latin **in order to** read ancient manuscripts and inscriptions.
4 b: Some cities, like Rome, have been inhabited for thousands of years **so** the ancient buildings are hidden below modern buildings.
5 d: In 79CE Pompeii was covered by a thick layer of volcanic ash from Mount Vesuvius. **As a result**, the city was particularly well preserved

⊙ 5

1 One of his greatest achievements was the building of the first Great Wall of China to protect China from its enemies. Not all of his achievements were military, however, as he <u>also</u> introduced a common form of writing throughout the country.
2 More than 700,000 workers and craftsmen took 38 years to complete the huge imperial palace, offices, and halls, all surrounded by a wall. <u>In addition</u>, the emperor ordered an army to be built so that his palace would be protected.

⊙ 6

1 Museums are important centres for research. <u>Moreover</u>, many have laboratories for preserving ancient objects.
2 Petra is of major historic significance <u>as well as</u> being a place of great beauty.
3 Studying history helps us to understand the past. <u>Furthermore</u>, it can help our understanding of the present.
4 Archaeological excavations often take a long time to complete. <u>What is more</u>, they can be very expensive.

⊙ 7

1 Museums need extensive funding for research and preserving objects. Furthermore, money is required to exhibit the objects properly and safely.
  Museums need extensive funding for research and preserving objects. Moreover, money is required to exhibit the objects properly and safely.
2 Machu Picchu is Peru's most important ancient monument. It is also one of the new seven wonders of the world.
  Machu Picchu is Peru's most important ancient monument as well as being one of the new seven wonders of the world.
3 The Hermitage Museum in St. Petersburg has over three million objects which visitors can admire. What is more, the collection can be seen on the museum's website.
  The Hermitage Museum in St. Petersburg has over three million objects which visitors can admire. In addition, the collection can be seen on the museum's website.

WRITING Museums pp48–49

AIMS
The aim of this section is to help students to improve their academic writing by checking their work for content and logical organization.

LEAD IN
- Ask:
  - *What is the topic of this section?* (museums)
  - *What museums have you been to?*
- Put the names of some museums on the board, e.g. the Louvre (Paris), the Hermitage (St. Petersburg), the British Museum (London), the Egyptian Museum (Cairo).
- Ask:
  - *Do you know these museums?*
  - *Has anyone visited them?*
- If any students have been, ask them to describe what they saw and what they thought about the museum.

PROCEDURE
1 Tell students to read the **Study Skill**. Explain that in academic writing (and particularly for exam essays) it is important for students to ensure that they have included all the necessary points and that the points are organized and linked in a logical manner.

   Students read the instructions and complete the task. Elicit the answers from the class. **O━ 1**

2 Students read the instructions and complete the task individually. Put students in pairs or small groups to compare their answers. Elicit the answers from the class. **O━ 2**

3 Students read the instructions and work in pairs to decide on the irrelevant sentence. Elicit answers from the class. If students have different ideas, ask them to explain why they think their choice of sentence is correct. **O━ 3**

Writing an evaluation essay p49

4 Put students into pairs or small groups to brainstorm ideas for the essay *The role of historic sites*. Elicit ideas and write them on the board.

   Students read the instructions. Tell them to decide what the purpose of the essay is (to evaluate). Ask students what a thesis statement should contain (see **Study Skill** p32). Students write the introductory paragraph. This could be set for homework. **O━ 4**

5 Students read the instructions. Students discuss the information in pairs. Elicit answers from the class. **O━ 5**

6 Students read the instructions and complete the task individually. If necessary, brainstorm with the whole class for examples. Students write the two paragraphs.

7 Students read the instructions and complete the task individually. Remind students to write their essays double-spaced to make correction easier.

8 Students read the instructions. Students check their work for purpose, content, and organization. **O━ 8**

EXTENSION ACTIVITY
Students should exchange their essays with a partner. Tell students to look for and mark errors in
- verb tenses
- prepositions
- missing words

Students work in pairs and explain the errors they have found to their partners. You may want to ask students to write a second draft of the essay incorporating the corrections.

WRITING Answer key pp48–49

O━ 1
1 To describe/evaluate museums.
2 Yes, but accept a 'no' answer if students can justify it.

O━ 2
Paragraph B: 1 yes 2 yes 3 yes
Paragraph C: 1 yes 2 yes 3 yes

O━ 3
Possible answers
Paragraph B:
The number of gold objects found in the tomb was extremely impressive.
Paragraph C:
There should be a text describing each object and its origins.

O━ 4
Model answer
This essay will describe the role of historic sites in today's society. It will describe the benefits these sites bring through education and tourism.

O━ 5
1 1.4 fun day out for the family
2 2.3 visitors take many photographs to show their friends

O━ 8
Model answer
Historic sites have an important role in teaching us how ancient people both worked and lived. For example, by visiting Baalbek in Lebanon, one can see what a Roman city centre looked like. Furthermore, other historic sites show us how ancient technologies were used to make tools, pottery, and jewellery. It is much easier for children to understand their country's history if they can see the sites rather than just read about them. In some places replicas have been built, for example, pottery kilns, so that children can make pots for themselves using the ancient technology. What is more, we can still learn a lot from these sites and technologies. For example, nobody has completely solved the engineering mystery of how the ancient Egyptians built the pyramids. This is something we still have to learn.

The second major benefit of historic sites is the fact that they encourage tourism. For example, more than 500,000 people visit Machu Picchu every year. Moreover, these visitors bring over $40m into the country every year. The money is generated because visitors need to spend on accommodation, transport, and food. Consequently, the economy of the area around an historic site benefits from increased employment, services, and sales, as does the national economy. A further benefit is that these visitors leave knowing more about the country's history and with a greater understanding of its culture.

In conclusion, it is clear that historic sites have an important role to play in a country in terms of educating that country's own population, as well as teaching visitors about its history and culture. These sites have an equally important role in improving the local and national economy as a result of tourist spending.

VOCABULARY DEVELOPMENT Collocations (2) p50

AIMS
The aim of this section is to make students aware of collocations, that is, those groups of words that frequently appear together. Recognizing and using common collocations will help students to read more quickly and to produce more natural-sounding written work.

LEAD IN
- Ask:
  - *What is a collocation?* (See Teacher's Guide p22)
  - *How are collocations formed?* (See Teacher's Guide p22)

PROCEDURE

1 Students read the **Study Skill** and the instructions. Students work in pairs to identify the collocations. Elicit answers from the class. **⌗ 1**

2 Students read the instructions and complete the task, working individually. Put students into pairs to compare answers. **⌗ 2**

3 Students read the instructions and complete the task individually. Remind students that they should always read the example sentences of words they are looking up in a dictionary. These often show collocations. Students compare their answers in pairs or small groups. Check answers with the whole class. **⌗ 3**

4 Students read the instructions and complete the task. Elicit the answers from the class. **⌗ 4**

Tell students to use their dictionaries to find out how collocations are written. Some are two separate words and some are hyphenated.

5 Students read the instructions and complete the task, working individually. Check the answers with the whole class. **⌗ 5**

VOCABULARY DEVELOPMENT Answer key p50

⌗ 1

damaged extensively, destroyed completely, search methodically

⌗ 2

1 The students <u>listened attentively</u> to Dr Potter's lecture on the excavations at Leptis Magna.
2 Our knowledge of how ancient people lived has <u>improved enormously</u> with the use of new technology such as Global Positioning Systems (GPS).
3 The fire in the museum <u>spread rapidly</u> and caused extensive damage.
4 This essay will <u>concentrate mainly</u> on the events of August 1705.
5 The scientific methods used in archaeology today <u>contrast sharply</u> with the methods used in the 19th century.

⌗ 3

1 felt strongly	2 remember correctly
3 expanded significantly	4 discovered by chance
5 benefit enormously	6 describe precisely

⌗ 4

Excavations are often carried out by <u>highly-qualified</u> teams of archaeologists helped by local volunteers or workers. Although the work is often <u>painstakingly slow</u>, it can produce fascinating results.

⌗ 5

1 cautiously optimistic	2 clearly illustrated
3 fully-equipped	4 actively encouraged
5 widely available	6 further complicated

REVIEW p51

AIMS

The aims of this section are to give students further practice in the skills learnt in this unit, and to give them the opportunity to review the work they have done. A further aim is to encourage students to apply what they have learnt to their academic studies in English.

PROCEDURE

1 Students read the instructions and complete the task. Put students into pairs to discuss the answers. Check the answers with the whole class. **⊙ 1**

2 Students read the instructions and complete the task working in pairs. Copy the table onto the board. Ask some students to come up and write in the collocations from the text. **⊙ 2**

3 Students read the instructions and complete the task, working in pairs. Discuss the answers with the whole class. **⊙ 3**

4 Students read the instructions and complete the task. You may wish to set this exercise for homework. **⊙ 4**

REVIEW Answer key p51

⊙ 1

The majestic ruins of the ancient city of Sabratha lie about 80km west of Tripoli, the capital of Libya. They are the high point of any visit to that country.
It is thought that the original settlement started in the 4th century BCE. However, by the second century BCE, Sabratha was a thriving city. Its success was based on trade across the Mediterranean and south into Africa for animals and ivory.
In the first century CE, there was a violent earthquake. **(a) As a result, many buildings were destroyed and the city had to be rebuilt.** In the 200 years which followed, the city expanded steadily and became increasingly wealthy. **(c) What is more, it became an important regional centre.** However, when it suffered another earthquake in 365 CE, the buildings simply collapsed. **(b) This was because they had been built of very soft sandstone.**
This time the city never really recovered. It was occupied by various armies until it was abandoned in the 8th century CE. It was rediscovered in the 20th century CE by archaeologists. Since then some of the major buildings, such as the theatre have been reconstructed and many pieces of artwork have been uncovered. **(d) These include magnificent mosaics and statues.** These can be seen in the nearby museum.

⊙ 2

adjective + noun: majestic ruins, ancient city, original settlement, thriving city, violent earthquake, major buildings
adverb + adjective: increasingly wealthy
verb + adverb: expanded steadily

⊙ 3

1 to give a (brief) description of Machu Picchu / to describe Machu Picchu
2 no – no reference to 3.2 religious/cultural – possible?
3 yes
4 not all

⊙ 4

This essay will give a brief description of the Inca city of Machu Picchu, in modern day Peru. It will argue that this ancient city is one of the most important archaeological sites in South America. Machu Picchu is a city located high up in the Andes mountains in Peru. It is an incredibly beautiful location. **(2)** It was built between 1460 and 1470 CE by an Inca ruler.
It is unlikely that it had any military or commercial functions because it was built so high up and in a fairly inaccessible place. What is more, there is no archaeological or written evidence that it was an administrative centre. **It is, therefore, more likely that it had some religious or cultural function. (1)**

There are about 200 buildings at Machu Picchu, including houses, storage structures, temples, and other public buildings. (3) It is clear that they were planned and constructed with great care and precision. The buildings are made of an extremely hard stone, yet they fit on top of one another perfectly. In fact, they fit so perfectly that it is impossible to put a thin knife blade between the stones. This feat of construction has led archaeologists to speculate about the type of tools which could have been used to cut the stone so perfectly.

7 Wonders of the modern world

READING Feats of engineering pp52–53

AIMS

The aim of this section is to make reading easier for students by helping them to deal with unknown words, complex sentences, and referents.

LEAD IN

- Focus students' attention on the page. Ask students to identify the skill READING, and the topic (*Feats of engineering*). Elicit the meaning of the title (something that demands great engineering skills) by drawing students' attention to the pictures.

PROCEDURE

1 Students read the instructions. Give students two minutes to discuss the answers in pairs or small groups. Elicit answers from the class. **⊶ 1**

2 Students read the instructions. Give students 30 seconds to complete the task. Elicit the answers. **⊶ 2**

3 Students read the instructions. Give the students three minutes to complete the task. Students compare answers in pairs. Elicit the answers. **⊶ 3**

4 Students read the instructions and complete the task. Students compare answers in pairs. **⊶ 4**

5 Students read the **Study Skill**. Students read the instructions and complete the task individually. Students compare answers in pairs. Elicit the answers. **⊶ 5**

6 Students read the **Study Skill**. Students read the instructions and complete the task individually. Students compare answers in pairs. Ask some students to tell the class their answers. **⊶ 6**

7 Students read the instructions and complete the task individually. Students compare answers in pairs. Get three students to write the answers on the board. **⊶ 7** p43

READING Answer key pp52–54

⊶ 1 Students' own answers.

⊶ 2 towers, a bridge, a dam

⊶ 3

1 in the city of Kuala Lumpur, in Malaysia   2 452 metres
3 2004   4 120 years   5 Parana   6 50 million tons

⊶ 4

1 They have 1,800 square metres of office space on every floor, a shopping centre, a concert hall, double-decker lifts, glass and steel sunshades.
2 The Muslim culture of Malaysia
3 It was built to relieve the city's congestion problems.
4 It is the world's highest bridge, over 340m, and breathtakingly beautiful. It is supported by seven concrete and steel pillars which rise into seven graceful pylons which can withstand extreme seismic and meteorological conditions.
5 In 1995 it produced 78% of the energy needs of Paraguay and 25% of Brazil's needs, breaking previous records for energy production.
6 The amount of iron and steel used was equivalent to over 300 Eiffel Towers, the volume of concrete needed was equal to 210 football stadiums, the course of the seventh biggest river in the world was changed, and 50 million tons of earth and rock were removed.

⊶ 5

inaugurated: verb (past participle), opened
slender: adjective, thin
breathtakingly: adverb, extremely
withstand: verb, to be strong enough not to break
joint: adjective, shared or owned by two or more people
course: noun, route or direction

⊶ 6

1 It is an impossible task to select the most amazing wonders of the modern world, since every year more wonderful constructions appear.
2 The Petronas Towers were the tallest buildings in the world when they were inaugurated in 1999.
3 Constructed of high-strength concrete, the building provides around 1800 square metres of office space on every floor, and includes a shopping centre and a concert hall at the base.
4 Described as one of the most breathtakingly beautiful bridges in the world, it was built to relieve the city's congestion problems caused by traffic passing from Paris en route to Barcelona, in Spain.
5 The bridge is supported by seven concrete and steel pillars which rise into seven graceful pylons.
6 In 1995 it produced 78% of Paraguay's and 25% of Brazil's energy needs, breaking previous records for energy production.

Islands in the sun p54

LEAD IN

- Write the title of the page (*Islands in the sun*) on the board. Ask:
  - *What is an island?* (land surrounded by water)
  - *What islands have you visited?*

PROCEDURE

8 Students read the instructions. Students discuss the answers in pairs or in small groups. Elicit the answers. **⊶ 8**

9 Students read the instructions. Give students two minutes to complete the task. Elicit the answers. **⊶ 9**

10 Students read the instructions and complete the task individually. Elicit the answers and ask students to correct the false statements. **⊶ 10**

11 Students read the **Study Skill**. Students complete the task in pairs or in small groups. Ask some students to tell the class their answers. **⊶ 11**

⊶ 7

1 It is an impossible task to select the most amazing wonders of the modern world, since every year more wonderful constructions appear.
2 The bridge is supported by seven concrete and steel pillars which rise into seven graceful pylons.
3 Designed by the British architect Norman Foster and constructed by a French company, it was built to withstand the most extreme seismic and meteorological conditions and is guaranteed for 120 years!

⊶ 8

Possible answers
1 oil rigs, lighthouses, sea walls
2 to search for oil/gas, to warn ships of coastline/rocks, to protect the coast from erosion

⊶ 9

1 the Palm Islands, the World Islands
2 building of artificial islands
3 Dubai, in the United Arab Emirates (UAE).

⊶ 10

1 True
2 False (the water is not very deep)
3 NS
4 True
5 NS
6 False (it will be larger than the city of Paris)

⊶ 11

They (line 3): the Palm Islands
This (line 16): the large crescent shape, made from rocks and sand, which protects the islands
It (line 22): the fact that all the houses were sold within three days
it (line 30): the construction of Palm Deira
These (line 33): the facilities – marinas, shopping malls, sports facilities, and clubs

VOCABULARY DEVELOPMENT
Word-building (1) p55

AIMS

The aim of this section is to make students aware of common suffixes. Recognizing suffixes will help students to read more quickly and will increase their vocabulary.

LEAD IN

- Dictate these words to the students:
  describe, description, descriptive, descriptively
- Elicit what these words are (different parts of speech of the same word – verb, noun, adjective, and adverb). Elicit how the words differ from each other (different suffixes or endings).

PROCEDURE

1 Students read the **Study Skill**. Students read the instructions and complete the task individually. Ask some students to write the answers on the board. Ask students to identify the suffix. 🔑 1

2 Students read the instructions and complete the task individually. Students compare answers with a partner. Point out to the students that in some cases there is more than one possible answer for one part of speech. Ask some students to write the answers on the board with the word stress. Make sure the students pronounce the word with the correct stress.

verb	noun	adjective	adverb
analyse	analysis analyst	analytical	analytically
	(in)consistency	(in)consistent	(in)consistently
decide	decision decisiveness	(in)decisive	(in)decisively
economize	economist economy economics	economical economic	economically
invent	invention inventor	inventive	*inventively*
involve	involvement	involved	
produce	product production produce	productive	productively
signify	(in)significance	(in)significant	(in)significantly
theorize	theory theorist	theoretical	theoretically

3 Students read the instructions and complete the task individually. Students compare answers in pairs. Elicit the answers. 🔑 3

4 Students read the instructions and complete the task individually. Students compare answers in pairs. Elicit the answers. 🔑 4

EXTENSION ACTIVITY

Students choose five words from their field of study and find the parts of speech. They mark the stress and then present them to the class.

VOCABULARY DEVELOPMENT Answer key p55

🔑 1

addition	noun	impressive	adjective
archaeologist	noun	innovative	adjective
artificial	adjective	remarkable	adjective
breathtakingly	adverb	residential	adjective
conclusion	noun	seismic	adjective
efficiently	adverb	successfully	adverb
expensively	adverb	unnecessarily	adverb
experiment	noun		

🔑 3

1 analysis
2 consistently
3 decision
4 economics
5 involve
6 productive
7 inventor
8 (in)significantly
9 theory

🔑 4

1 inaugurated
2 innovative
3 installed
4 length
5 exceptionally
6 impressive

RESEARCH Crediting sources (1) p56

AIMS
The aims of this section are to raise students' awareness of the importance of crediting sources.

LEAD IN
- Ask:
  - *Where do you find the information you need for your studies?* (in books, encyclopaedias, journals, on the Internet)
  - *If you use information from such sources, what must you do to avoid plagiarism?* (credit the source/acknowledge the source)

PROCEDURE
Tell students to read the **Study Skill**. Students read the instructions and complete the task individually. Students compare answers in pairs. Give the students plenty of time to check their answers. Ask a student to write the answers on the board.

BACKGROUND INFORMATION
The APA (American Psychological Association) style has been used throughout this book for crediting sources as it is the preferred style in many universities for social sciences. However, it is only one example style and you may wish to ask students to do the task in their department's style. Whichever style is used, students must pay great attention to detail including the order and punctuation, and if they are writing their work electronically, spacing and the use of italics.

RESEARCH Answer key p56

Matache, A. (2005) *Building in Challenging Environments*. Canberra: Wexford University Press.

Sinden, J. (2004). The cost of construction. *The Journal of General Structural Engineering, 4*, 34–56.

Smallridge, J. *Artificial Islands*. Retrieved September 4, 2006, from http://www./ulid.man.ac.uk/islandmanagement/

LANGUAGE FOR WRITING
Verbs for reporting another writer's ideas p56

AIMS
The aim of this section is help students to recognize and use fixed phrases and linking words that are commonly used in academic writing.

LEAD IN
Ask students to think of some verbs which are used in reported speech, apart from *say* and *tell*. Write these verbs on the board and check that students understand their differences in meaning.

PROCEDURE
1 Students read the instructions. Students work individually and compare answers with a partner. **⊶ 1**

2 Students read the **Rules** and the instructions. Tell students that more then one answer may be possible. Students work individually and then discuss their answers in pairs or in small groups. Elicit the different possible answers. **⊶ 2**

ADDITIONAL PHOTOCOPIABLE ACTIVITY
Writing 7 Writing a summary

LANGUAGE FOR WRITING Answer key p56

⊶ 1

In this article from the website <u>wondersoftheworld.com</u>, the writer presents three different structures that, he <u>argues</u>, should be considered as wonders of the modern world. These three structures have been built in different parts of the world for very different purposes, but all three are amazing for their innovative design, beauty, and size. The author first <u>describes</u> the Petronas Towers in Malaysia. These twin towers were the highest in the world when they were built, dominating the city of Kuala Lumpur. The second construction chosen is the Millau Bridge in France. The writer <u>explains</u> that this bridge was built to reduce the traffic problems in the city, but, because of its beauty, it has become a tourist attraction itself. The third construction is the Itaipu Dam in Paraguay. This huge dam was built on the river between Paraguay and Brazil, and is used to provide water for an enormous hydroelectric power plant.

⊶ 2

The most wonderful islands is an article which (1) **describes** the artificial islands in the UAE. Taken from the website 'wondersoftheworld.com', it (2) **argues/claims** that the Palm Islands are one of the wonders of the modern world. The writer (3) **describes/explains** how these islands were constructed and why they were built. There are three islands being constructed in the sea from sand and rocks. Each one will have tourist attractions as well as luxurious accommodation. The author (4) **claims/believes/argues** that these islands are true feats of modern engineering.

WRITING Tunnels and buildings pp57–58

AIMS
The aim of this section is to give students practice in summarizing, from complex sentences to simple ones, from paragraphs to one or two sentences, and from texts to short summaries.

LEAD IN
- Dictate or write the following sentence on the board:
The climatic conditions in the United Kingdom are the object of a great deal of discussion and are commonly the most talked about subject when people, who may or may not know each other, meet.
- Ask:
  – *Can you simplify this sentence into one main idea?* (People in the UK talk about the weather.)

PROCEDURE

1 Students read the instructions and complete the task individually. Students compare answers in pairs. Elicit the answers. Ask why the other answers are incorrect (they omit important information). **⊶1**

2 Tell students to read the **Study Skill**. Students read the instructions and complete the task individually. Remind students to only underline the essential information. Students compare answers with a partner. Elicit the answers. **⊶2**

3 Students read the instructions and complete the task individually. Ask some students to read their answers aloud. Choose two or three and write them on the board. Ask the class to vote on which one is best. If they disagree, ask them to explain why. **⊶3**

4 Students read the instructions and complete the task individually. Elicit the answers. **⊶4**

5 Students read the instructions and organize the ideas. Encourage students to compare their answers. Students write their sentences individually and compare their answers. Ask some students to read their answers aloud. Choose two or three and write them on the board. Ask the class to vote on which one is best. If they disagree, ask them to explain why. **⊶5**

6 Students read the instructions and complete the task. Encourage the students to underline the main ideas in the text. **⊶6**

Writing a summary p58

7 Students read the instructions and complete the task individually. **⊶7**

EXTENSION ACTIVITY
Ask the students to write a summary of a text from their own field of study. Remind them to use words and phrases from the *Language for Writing* section.

WRITING Answer key pp57–58

⊶1 1b 2a 3b

⊶2
Possible answers
A Many countries in the world have a growing population, and in some countries the population is increasing by as much as two per cent every decade. This population expansion results in an increase in the demand for housing, and causes overcrowding.
B One of the most noticeable phenomena in many of today's large capital cities is their increasingly efficient public transport systems. These encourage people to leave their privately-owned vehicles at home.
C High-rise buildings are now common in our big cities. These skyscrapers are seen as a solution to the shortage of available land because by building vertically rather than horizontally, more accommodation can be obtained from the same surface area.

⊶3
Model answers
A The increasing population in many countries in the world causes a rise in demand for accommodation and causes overcrowding.
B An effective public transport network results in decreased use of private cars in many capital cities.
C Skyscrapers can solve the problem of a shortage of land for housing.

⊶4
Possible answers
Due to an increase in traffic between the various islands which make up Japan, and predictions of a continuing growth in train travel, a rail tunnel was built to connect the islands of Honshu and Hokkaido. The Seikan Tunnel in Japan is today the longest railway tunnel in the world, with a length of almost 54 km. When the tunnel was opened in 1988, … However, newer Japanese bullet trains have never used the tunnel because of the cost of extending the high-speed line through it. … This, combined with a fall in the cost of flying, … tunnel is not used as much as forecasters had predicted.

⊶5 Model answer
The longest railway tunnel in the world links the islands of Honshu and Hokkaido in Japan. This 54km tunnel was inaugurated in 1988 to deal with the predicted increase in rail traffic. However, the fall in the cost of flying and the fact that high-speed trains cannot use the tunnel have resulted in the tunnel being less widely used than expected.

⊶6 Possible answers
The Sydney Opera House is one of the most famous architectural wonders of the modern world. Instantly recognizable both for its roof shells and its impressive location in Sydney Harbour, …
… this large performing arts centre was started in 1959 and completed in 1973. … The Opera House includes five theatres, five rehearsal studios, two main halls, four restaurants, six bars, and several shops.
… It was expected to cost $7 million, but in fact, the final cost was $102 million. …
It was inaugurated by Queen Elizabeth II on 20th October 1973, …

⊶7 Model answer
The Sydney Opera House, which has been described as one of the wonders of the modern world, is located in Sydney, Australia. Designed by the Danish architect, Jorn Utzo, this large performing arts centre with numerous theatres, restaurants, and other facilities took fourteen years to build at a cost of over $100 million dollars. It is claimed that the high cost of construction was due to adverse weather conditions, difficulties encountered with the design, and problems with the contract. Expected to have been completed by 1963, it was finally inaugurated by Queen Elizabeth II in 1973 at a ceremony which was televised to millions of viewers. (106 words)

AIMS

The aims of this section are to give students further practice in the skills learnt in this unit, and to give them the opportunity to review the work they have done. A further aim is to encourage students to apply what they have learnt to their academic studies in English.

PROCEDURE

1 Students read the instructions and complete the task individually. Students compare answers in pairs. Elicit the answers. **⊶ 1**

2 Students read the instructions. You may wish to refer students back to the **Study Skill** on p53. Ask some of the students to write their answers on the board. Encourage students to mark the word stress. Check that they know that *debris* is an uncountable noun. **⊶ 2**

3 Students read the instructions and complete the task. Elicit the answers. **⊶ 3**

4 Students read the instructions. They complete the task individually and then compare answers in pairs. **⊶ 4**

5 Students read the instructions. Remind students to identify the main ideas, to organize these logically, and to use their own words. Students complete the task individually. Ask one or two students to read out their summaries. Write some on the board and ask the class to vote on the best one. **⊶ 5**

6 Elicit from students some suffixes for the parts of speech (see **Study Skill** p55). Students read the instructions and complete the task. Remind students to mark the stress. **⊶ 6**

EXTENSION ACTIVITY

Ask the students to list the skills they have learnt and practised in this unit. For example:
– dealing with unknown words, complex sentences and referents
– word-building – suffixes
– crediting sources
– reporting another writer's words
– summarizing

Put students into small groups to discuss how they could apply these skills to their academic studies.

REVIEW Answer key p59

⊶ 1

1 a space station, built to show that people could spend long periods of time in space and to observe the solar system
2 from 1973 to 1975, 3 missions
3 sustained severe damage, but this was repaired
4 medical experiments, investigations into gravitational effects, and solar observations
5 atmospheric changes caused it to crash-land in 1979

⊶ 2

word	part of speech	your guess
launched	verb	to send into the sky
orbit	noun	curved path around a planet
solar	adjective	connected with the sun
sustained	verb	to experience something bad
crew	noun	people who work on a ship/plane
mission	noun	a special journey
gravitational	adjective	connected to gravity
debris	noun	pieces of something that has been destroyed

⊶ 3

1 Helped by ground control, the crew managed to repair this damage during a spacewalk, and the mission continued.
2 In total there were three Skylab missions between 1973 and 1975, during which time many scientific studies were carried out.
3 It crash-landed in Australia in 1979, spreading its debris over a large area.

⊶ 4

It (line 2): Skylab
which (line 4): observations
it (line 5): Skylab
These (line 8): scientific studies
its (line 13): Skylab's

⊶ 5

Model answer
Skylab was a space station which was launched in 1973 to enable scientists to carry out experiments in space. After three missions, Skylab was left orbiting in space, but it crashed onto the Earth in 1979.

⊶ 6

verb	noun	adjective	adverb
complete	completion	complete	completely
differ	difference	different	differently
observe	observer	observant	observantly
	observation		
prove	proof	proven	–
–	science	scientific	scientifically
succeed	success	successful	successfully

8 Olympic business

READING SKILLS Making notes
RESEARCH Avoiding plagiarism (3) and (4)
LANGUAGE FOR WRITING Expressing contrast
WRITING SKILLS Process writing • Writing a discursive essay
VOCABULARY DEVELOPMENT Synonyms and antonyms

READING The Olympic Games pp60–61

AIMS
The aims of this section are to make students aware of different ways of making notes, and to give them practice in using these different ways.

LEAD IN
- Focus students' attention on the page. Ask students to identify the skill READING, and the topic (*The Olympic Games*). Ask:
  – *Which cities have held the Olympic Games recently?* (Sydney, Athens, Beijing)
  – *Where will the next Games be held?*

PROCEDURE
1 Students read the instructions and complete the task. Students discuss answers in pairs or small groups for three minutes. Elicit answers from the class. **⊙1**

2 Students read the instructions. Give students two minutes to complete the task. Elicit the answers. **⊙2**

3 Students read the instructions, complete the task, then compare answers in pairs. **⊙3**

4 Students read the instructions. Give the students three minutes to complete the task. Students compare their answers in pairs. Elicit the answers. **⊙4**

5 Students read the instructions and complete the task individually. Students compare answers in pairs. Copy the diagram onto the board and ask some students to complete the diagram. **⊙5**

6 Students read the instructions and complete the task individually. Students compare answers in pairs. Elicit the answers. Students then read the **Study Skill**. Encourage discussion of the different ways of making notes. **⊙6**

Two Olympic bids p62

7 Students read the instructions and complete the task individually. Give students two minutes. Students compare answers in pairs. Elicit the answers. **⊙7**

8 Students read the instructions. Students do the task individually and compare answers in pairs. Draw the table on the board. Ask one or two students to complete the table.

	Rockley	Woodville
overall budget	3.5 billion	3.2 billion
capital costs	650m	700m
operating costs	1.5 billion	1.4 billion
transport upgrade	700m	600m
overheads & unexpected costs	650m	500m
government funding	1.6 billion	200m
regional funding	360m	200m
city funding	140m	800m
TV rights	750m	900m
ticket sales	150m	300m
sponsorship	500m	100m

9 Students read the instructions. Students discuss their answers in pairs or small groups. Elicit the answers. **⊙9**

READING Answer key pp60–62

⊙1
1 The rings represent the five continents in the world.
2–4 Students' own answers.

⊙2
1 G 2 F 3 A 4 C, D, E 5 B

⊙3
1 i 2 e 3 a 4 h 5 b 6 d 7 j 8 k 9 c 10 g 11 f

⊙4
1 tourists and students
2 sponsorships, advertising revenues, and TV/broadcasting rights
3 Their lives could be disrupted because of the large numbers of visitors and increased taxes.

⊙5
Advantages: world-class facilities, accommodation, transport system, more jobs
Disadvantages: serious disruption to daily lives, increased taxes, temporary unskilled jobs are created

⊙6
1 **Requirements**
  1.1 Sports facilities
  1.2 Accommodation
  1.3 Efficient & sufficient transport system
  1.4 Funding
  1.5 Security arrangements
2 **Funding**
  2.1 Sponsors
  2.2 Advertising revenues
  2.3 Broadcasting rights
3 **Conclusion**
  3.1 Host city gains overall in facilities and infrastructure
  3.2 Host city becomes an important place

⊙7
They are all emails giving financial information about a bid for hosting the Winter Olympic Games.

⊙9
Possible answers
1 Woodville predicts lower overheads and operating costs. It will have less funding from the government and region, but much more from the city. It also expects more money from TV rights and ticket sales, and much less from sponsorship.
2 Rockley's bid seems more realistic as it would be better to have more funding from the government and from sponsorship rather than from the city. Woodville's ticket sales seem rather optimistic.

RESEARCH   Crediting sources (2) p63

AIMS
The aim of this section is to give students practice in acknowledging/crediting sources and in using direct and indirect quotations.

LEAD IN
- Ask:
  - *What is plagiarism?* (see **Study Skill** on p14)
  - *How can you avoid plagiarism?* (by rephrasing, or crediting sources)

PROCEDURE

1 Students read the **Study Skill**. If your university has a set style for references, this section may be omitted and work on the department's own style can replace it. Students read the instructions and complete the task individually. Students compare answers in pairs. Elicit the answers. ⌐**1**

2 Students read the instructions and complete the task individually. Students compare answers in pairs. Elicit the answers. ⌐**2**

3 Tell students to read the **Study Skill**. Students read the instructions and complete the task individually. Students compare answers in pairs. Ask students to write the answers on the board. ⌐**3**

RESEARCH   Answer key p63

⌐**1**

(Matache, 2009)
(Sinden, 2007, p. 487)

⌐**2**

1 1 Haggeg
2 (2006)
3 (p. 52)

⌐**3**

2 Khalil (2003) claims, "hosting large events usually leaves the host city with large bills" (p. 54).
3 As Li Chung wrote (2006), "the opportunity for development is considerable" (p. 71).
4 Neal (2001) said, "transport upgrades are inevitable" (p. 268).

LANGUAGE FOR WRITING   Expressing contrast p64

AIMS

The aim of this section is to help students to recognize and use fixed phrases and linking words that are commonly used in academic writing.

PROCEDURE

1 Students read the instructions. Students work individually and compare answers in pairs. 🔑 1

2 Students read the **Rules**.

NB Tell the students that some of the words and phrases of contrast (*despite, in spite of, although, even though*) can come in the middle of the sentence.

Students read the instructions and complete the task. Elicit the answers from the class. 🔑 2

3 Students read the instructions and complete the task individually. Students compare answers in pairs. Elicit answers and draw students' attention to the punctuation. 🔑 3

LANGUAGE FOR WRITING   Answer key p64

🔑 1

1 … <u>However</u>, there are disadvantages to holding the Games.
2 … <u>although</u> there are disadvantages to holding the Olympic Games, it is generally agreed that the host city gains overall in terms of improvements in facilities and infrastructure.

🔑 2

1d   2c   3a   4b

🔑 3

1 Although it costs a huge amount of money to fund the Games, many cities compete to hold them.
2 Despite the Olympic Organizing Committee raising a large amount of money to fund the Games, huge debts remained after the Games.
3 The majority of the population were in favour of hosting the event. Nevertheless, there was opposition to the tax increases.
4 In spite of raising considerable sums of money through advertising, the football club did not have sufficient funds to construct a new stadium.
5 The team had not played together for very long. However, they won the game.
6 Even though the event was broadcast on national television, ten per cent of the population were unaware it was taking place.

WRITING A permanent site for the Olympics p65

AIMS
The aim of this section is to give students practice in writing from notes, including quotations in their writing, and following the whole process of writing as covered in Units 1–7.

LEAD IN
- Ask:
  - *Where were the first Olympics held?* (Greece)
  - *Where are they held now?* (different countries in the world)

PROCEDURE

1 Students read the instructions. Refer students to the **Study Skills** on p25 and p61. Elicit or give one example (e.g. impossible to choose one city) and write it on the board. Students do the task in pairs or small groups. Elicit the answers. Write the suggestions on the board in no particular order.

Ask students to recall what a thesis statement is (see **Study Skill** on p32). Students do the task in pairs or small groups. Ask some students to read their answers aloud. Choose two or three and write them on the board. Ask the class to vote on which one is best. If they disagree, ask them to explain why.

Refer the students to their suggestions on the board. Elicit how the notes could be organized (arguments *for* and *against*). Refer students to the **Study Skill** on p41. Students do the task in pairs or small groups. Elicit answers.

2 Students read the instructions and do the task individually. Ask some students which quotations they have chosen.

ADDITIONAL PHOTOCOPIABLE ACTIVITY
Writing 8 Internet research task

Writing a discursive essay p65

3 Students read the instructions. Ask students to recall what goes into an introduction, body paragraphs, and the conclusion. Refer them to the **Study Skills** on p32, p20, and p33. Students do the task individually. **⊶ 3**

4 Students read the instructions. Refer them to the **Study Skills** on pages 33, 48, 9, and 11 if necessary. Students do the task individually, or as peer correction (see Teacher's Guide p9). **⊶ 4**

5 Students read the instructions and do the task individually. Students read the **Study Skill**. **⊶ 5**

WRITING Answer key p65

⊶ 1

Possible ideas

Financial: costs less money to have a permanent site, no expensive bidding process every four years

Facilities: can be constantly improved on

Unfair pressure on the inhabitants of the place where the Games are permanently held

Unfair financial advantages to one city

Impossible to choose one city

Important to have Games in different countries and continents so that a variety of places share prestige/significance

Model thesis statements

The Olympic Games are held every four years in a different host city. This essay will put forward arguments why the Games should have a permanent site.

The Olympic Games are held every four years in a different host city. This essay will explain why it is important that different countries should host the Games each time.

Possible arguments

For: costs less money to have permanent site, no expensive bidding process every four years, facilities can be constantly improved on,

Against: unfair pressure on the inhabitants of one city, unfair financial advantages for one city, impossible to choose one city, variety of places share significance and prestige.

⊶ 2

Students' own answers.

⊶ 3

Students' own answers.

⊶ 4

Students' own answers.

⊶ 5

Students' own answers.

VOCABULARY DEVELOPMENT   Synonyms p66

AIMS
The aim of this section is to make students aware of synonyms and antonyms and the different contexts in which they can or cannot be used.

LEAD IN
- Write these sentences on the board. Ask:
  – *Are the underlined words correct in these sentences? If not, why not?*
    a The department is planning to <u>have</u> a meeting on Monday.
    b The department is planning to <u>hold</u> a meeting on Monday.
    c The students <u>have</u> exams at the end of each term.
    d The students <u>hold</u> exams at the end of each term.
- Elicit from the students that d is not correct as the context is wrong.

PROCEDURE
1 Students read the **Study Skill**. Students read the instructions and complete the task individually. Elicit the answers. 🔑 1

2 Students read the instructions and complete the task individually. Students compare answers in pairs. Elicit the answers. 🔑 2

Antonyms p66

LEAD IN
- Dictate these words to the students:
  light   old   hard
- Ask the students to write the opposites of the words.
  light ≠ dark/heavy
  old ≠ new/modern
  hard ≠ easy/soft
- Ask:
  – *What do you notice about these opposite words?* (sometimes a word has more than one opposite)

PROCEDURE
3 Students read the **Study Skill**. Students read the instructions and complete the task individually. Students compare answers in pairs. Elicit the answers. 🔑 3

4 Students read the instructions and complete the task individually. Students compare answers in pairs. Elicit the answers. 🔑 4

EXTENSION ACTIVITY
Ask students to find synonyms and antonyms from their field of study and present them to the class.

VOCABULARY DEVELOPMENT   Answer key p66

🔑 **1**
1 d The footballer gained over one million euros last year.
2 c The student borrowed the finance to fund his studies.
3 b The winner increased his arm to salute the spectators.

🔑 **2**
1 sponsor
2 raised
3 gain
4 increased
5 earn
6 supported

🔑 **3**
1 ~~normal~~   2 ~~even~~   3 ~~weak~~   4 ~~slight~~

🔑 **4**
1 blunt   2 dull   3 Compulsory   4 paid   5 loud   6 hard

AIMS

The aims of this section are to give students further practice in the skills learnt in this unit, and to give them the opportunity to review the work they have done. A further aim is to encourage students to apply what they have learnt to their academic studies in English.

PROCEDURE

1 Students read the instructions. Ask students to recall different ways of making notes (mind map, linear notes, table). Students then complete the task individually. Students compare answers in pairs. Elicit the answers. **⊶ 1**

2 Students read the instructions and complete the task individually. Refer students back to the **Study Skill** on p63 if necessary. You may wish to give the students some page numbers to add to their direct quotations as this would be the correct APA style. For example; Foster – p42, FIFA – p81, Brown – p11. **⊶ 2**

3 Students read the instructions and complete the task individually. Ask a student to write the answers on the board. Students can rewrite the sources in their department's style if preferred. **⊶ 3**

4 Students read the instructions. Remind students to refer to the **Rules** on p64. Students do the task individually. Students compare answers in pairs. Elicit the answers. Remind the students about the punctuation. **⊶ 4**

5 Students read the instructions. Students complete the task individually. Students compare answers in pairs. Elicit the answers. **⊶ 5**

EXTENSION ACTIVITY

Ask the students to list the skills they have learnt and practised in this unit. For example:
– different ways of making notes
– crediting sources
– writing from notes
– ways of expressing contrast
– synonyms and antonyms

Put students into small groups to discuss how they could apply these skills to their academic studies.

⊶ 1

Possible answers
1   1.1   Different country each time.
    1.2   In past in Europe and Americas
    1.3   2010 was held in Africa

2
Winners of the World Cup	
Country	Number of times winner
Brazil	5
Italy	4
Germany	3
Argentina	2
Uruguay	2
France	1
England	1

3   3.1   First broadcast in 1954
    3.2   Most popular sports event on TV (more popular than the Olympic Games)
    3.3   30 billion people watched the 2006 World Cup
    3.4   715 million people watched the 2006 World Cup final
    3.5   41,100 hours of football broadcast on TV in 2006

⊶ 2

The World Cup was first broadcast on television in 1954 and is now the most popular televised sporting event in the world. It has been reported that "more spectators watch the event than the Olympic Games" (Foster, 1997, p. 42). The audience of the 2006 World Cup held in Germany was estimated to be almost 30 billion. According to FIFA (2010), the international governing body of football, "715 million people watched the final match of this tournament" (p. 81). Broadcasting this event resulted in 41,100 hours of football on TV across the world. Clearly, the World Cup matches attract huge audiences, but even the draws, which decide the distribution of teams into groups, are widely viewed. The 2010 World Cup draw was as Brown (2010) reported, "seen by 300 million people" (p. 11).

⊶ 3

a   2006 FIFA World Cup TV Coverage. Retrieved May 13, 2010, from www.fifa.com/en/marketing/concept/ondex
b   Smallridge, E. C. Hosting the Olympics. What remains? Retrieved January 2, 2006, from http://www.thejournalofaccounts.com
c   Foster, J. M. (1997). Watching sports events. Journal of Televised Events, 23, 32–45.
d   Brown, N. (2010) Football and television. International Review of Media, 65, 21–34.

⊶ 4

Possible answers
1   Despite having only met on one occasion, the committee organized the event very well.
2   Although the weather was very hot, the athlete broke the world record.
3   The tickets for the match were very expensive. However, they were all sold within a few hours.
4   In spite of the funds being sufficient for the event, the city was not chosen.
5   The chairman was appointed for four years. Nevertheless, he resigned after six months.

⊶ 5

	a		b
1	have		hosting
2	employ		rented
3	map		arrangements
4	complete		busy

9 Trends

READING Work pp68–69

AIMS

The aims of this section are to give students practice in interpreting visual information.

LEAD IN

• Focus students' attention on the page. Ask students to identify the skill READING, and the topic (*Work*).

PROCEDURE

1 Students read the instructions. Elicit what is meant by *sectors* (different types of business activities). Students discuss the answers in pairs or small groups for three minutes. Elicit answers from the class. **⊶1**

BACKGROUND INFORMATION

The term 'graphic' has been used in this unit to include line graphs, bar charts, pie charts, and tables. Bar charts can also be referred to as bar graphs.

2 Students read the **Study Skill**. Then they read the instructions and complete the task individually. Give students 30 seconds to complete the task. Elicit the answers. **⊶2**

3 Students read the instructions. Give the students three minutes to complete the task. Students compare answers in pairs. Elicit the answers. **⊶3**

4 Students read the instructions. Encourage students to use their own words, not simply read from the text. Students complete the task individually and compare answers in pairs. **⊶4**

5 Students read the instructions and complete the task individually. Students compare answers in pairs. Elicit the answers. **⊶5**

Trends in education p70

6 Students read the instructions and complete the task individually. Give the students one minute. Students compare answers in pairs. Elicit the answers. **⊶6**

BACKGROUND INFORMATION

The arts are subjects you study at school or university which are not scientific, such as language, literature, and history.

7 Students read the **Study Skill**. Students read the instructions and complete the task individually. Students compare answers with a partner. Elicit the answers.

EXTENSION ACTIVITY

For homework, ask the students to research on the Internet (see **Study Skill** on p23) statistics about employment sectors in their country. Students present this information as a graph and write a description of it.

READING Answer key pp68–70

⊶1
Possible answers
1 education, industry, health, services
2–4 Students' own answers.

⊶2
1 Figure 3   2 Figure 2   3 Figure 1

⊶3
1 Fig. 1: the percentage of the global workforce in the major sectors in 2005
   Fig. 2: the sectors of global employment between 1995 and 2005
   Fig. 3: the percentage of IT jobs in the service sector between 1994 and 2006
2 They are different types of graphs, and give different types of data.
3 The percentage is almost the same.
4 The services sector
5 It has risen steadily, but there was a slight fall in 1996.

⊶4
1 More machines were used, so fewer people were needed.
2 Generally the numbers of people employed in industry has fallen, but in some countries it has risen slightly.
3 The largest decrease in the number of employees in agriculture happened in South-East Asia. It decreased by 12%. Low wages and industrialization caused a rise in industrial employment.
4 It rose sharply from 1994 to 1995. In 1996 there was a slight drop due to a recession, and then it continued to rise steadily.
5 Computer technology has changed the way work is done. Means of production, distribution, and communication have all been altered.

⊶5
1 not nearly as many   2 slight   3 considerably
4 Five per cent   5 a decrease

⊶6
For women: arts in both years
For men: information technology in 2000–2001 and medicine & dentistry in 2006–2007

⊶7
1 nearly/just under   2 twice as many   3 the same
4 three-quarters   5 just over   6 just under/nearly

LANGUAGE FOR WRITING
Language for describing graphs, charts, and statistics pp71–72

AIMS
The aim of this section is help students recognize and use fixed phrases and linking words that are commonly used in academic writing.

PROCEDURE

1 Students read instructions. Refer students back to the **Study Skill** on p68 to help them. Students work individually and compare answers in pairs. ⟜1

2 Students read the instructions and complete the task individually. Students compare answers in pairs. Ask one or two students to write the answers on the board. You might wish to point out to students that *plummet* and *plunge* mean to fall suddenly and quickly from a high position, and *rocket* means to increase very suddenly and quickly. ⟜2

3 Students read the instructions and complete the task individually. Students compare answers in pairs. Elicit answers and ask students to note that the word stress changes on *decrease* and *increase* depending on whether they are verbs or nouns: *to incréase, an íncrease, to decréase, a décrease* ⟜3

4 Students read the instructions and complete the task individually. You may wish to tell students that a *dramatic* rise/fall is often a large change, but the words *dramatic or dramatically* also imply an unexpected or sudden change. ⟜4

5 Students read the instructions and complete the task in pairs or small groups. Elicit the answers. ⟜5

6 Remind students that approximations are frequently used to interpret data in academic writing. Refer students back to the **Study Skill** on p70 of the Student's Book. Students read the instructions and do the task in pairs or small groups. Elicit the answers. ⟜6

7 Students read the instructions and complete the task in pairs or small groups. Ask one or two students to write the answers on the board. ⟜7

8 Students read the instructions and complete the task individually. Students compare answers in pairs. Elicit the answers. ⟜8

ADDITIONAL PHOTOCOPIABLE ACTIVITY
Writing 9 Describing graphs and trends

LANGUAGE FOR WRITING Answer key pp71–72

⟜1
1 b The bar chart shows/illustrates the number of graduates who work in IT in different countries of the world.
2 c The line graph shows/illustrates the number of students in New Zealand between 1990 and 2005.
3 a The pie chart compares the percentage of graduates working in different sectors.

⟜2
rise: go up, soar, increase, rocket, grow
fall: plummet, decline, go down, plunge, decrease
stay the same: level out, stabilize
change frequently: fluctuate
peak: reach a peak

⟜3
a substantial fall
a considerable increase
a slight drop
a noticeable decrease
a marginal growth
a steady decline

⟜4

A large change	A small change
dramatically/dramatic	slightly/slight
considerably/considerable	marginally/marginal
noticeably/noticeable	steadily/steady

⟜5
2 Prices fell substantially and then ~~fluctuated~~ levelled out.
3 After a ~~slow~~ substantial/considerable rise there was a steady decline.
4 The value dropped and then levelled off for a while before ~~soaring~~ fluctuating.

⟜6
1 70% of   2 A quarter   3 90% of   4 Nearly two-thirds
5 47%

⟜7
The academic year 2006–2007 saw a general increase(in) student numbers as most faculties registered a rise(in) enrolments. For example, the number of men studying IT rose(from) 108 in 2000 (to) just over 140 in 2006, and numbers studying law rose(to) over 350 men and just under 200 women. There were some decreases. The number of men studying medicine and dentistry dropped(to) 130, and the number of women studying economics and commerce also fell(by) sixty,(to) 406.

⟜8
1 in   2 to   3 of   4 to   5 by   6 from   7 to

AIMS

The aim of this section is to give students practice in describing non-textual information.

LEAD IN

- Write the following words on the board:
  babyhood   middle age   childhood   adulthood   old age   adolescence
- Ask the students to put the words in order of age. Ask students which is the biggest group in their country.

PROCEDURE

1 Students read the instructions and complete the task in pairs or small groups. Elicit the answers. **⊶ 1**

2 Students read the instructions. Ask students to recall the main types of graph and what they are used for (see **Study Skill** p68). Students do the task in pairs or small groups. Elicit the answers. **⊶ 2**

3 Students read the instructions and complete the task in pairs or small groups. Elicit the answers. **⊶ 3**

4 Students read the **Study Skill**. Students read the instructions and complete the task individually. Students compare their answers in pairs. **⊶ 4**

5 Students read the instructions and complete the task in pairs or small groups. Encourage the students to discuss each others' graphs. Elicit their answers. **⊶ 5**

Writing a report using visual information p73

6 Students read the instructions and complete the task individually.

7 Students write their report. Encourage the students to check their work for mistakes, or ask students to peer correct.

EXTENSION ACTIVITY

Ask students to research the answers to exercise 1 of this section on the Internet (see **Study Skill** p23). Students write a report of the information they have found, presenting some of the data graphically.

⊶ 1
Students' own answers.

⊶ 2
1 a line graph
2 a pie chart
3 a bar chart

⊶ 3
Students might want to choose from Tables 1–3, but the information in Table 4 is irrelevant.

⊶ 4
Possible answers
Table 1: a bar chart showing all the data/two pie charts for 2002 and 2025
Table 2/3: a bar chart showing all the data/three pie charts by age group/four pie charts by region
A line graph is not appropriate for any of this data.

⊶ 5
Students' own answers.

⊶ 7
Students' own answers.

VOCABULARY DEVELOPMENT Word-building (2) p74

AIMS

The aim of this section is to make students aware of common prefixes. Recognizing how words are formed will help students to read more quickly and will increase their vocabulary.

LEAD IN

- Dictate these words to the students:

  act   react   action   reaction   reactive   reactivate

- Ask:
  – *What do these words have in common?* (all have the same stem or root)
  – *How do they differ?* (different prefixes and suffixes)

PROCEDURE

1 Students read the **Study Skill**. Students read the instructions and complete the task individually. Tell students there are no negative prefixes in this exercise. Elicit the answers. 🔑 **1**

BACKGROUND INFORMATION

Prefixes can be categorized under different general headings. This will help students understand and remember the meanings of the prefixes.

2 Students read the instructions and complete the task individually. Students compare answers with a partner. Elicit the answers. 🔑 **2**

3 Students read the instructions and complete the task individually. Students compare answers with a partner. Elicit the answers. 🔑 **3**

EXTENSION ACTIVITY

Ask students to write down the meanings of the prefixes in exercise 1. For example:

poly- = many/much

nano- = one billionth

VOCABULARY DEVELOPMENT Answer key p74

🔑 1

Number
poly- e.g. polyunsaturated	*multi-* e.g. multilingual
mono- e.g. monorail	*bi-* e.g. bilateral

Size
nano- e.g. nanogram	*micro-* e.g. microorganisms
kilo- e.g. kilometres	

Time
ante- e.g. antecedent	*post-* e.g. postgraduate
re- e.g. reread	*pre-* e.g. preview

Place
sub- e.g. subtitles	*inter-* e.g. international
intra- e.g. intranet	

Substance
hydro- e.g. hydroelectric	*bio-* e.g. biochemistry
photo- e.g. photosynthesis	

🔑 2

Negatives
1 *ir-* e.g. irregular	2 *in-* e.g. inefficient
3 *im-* e.g. imperfect	4 *dis-* e.g. disorganized
5 *un-* e.g. unsuitable	6 *il-* e.g. illegible

🔑 3

1 nanosecond
2 submarine
3 hydroplane
4 Prehistory
5 unreliable
6 bilingual

AIMS

The aims of this section are to give students further practice in the skills learnt in this unit, and to give them the opportunity to review the work they have done. A further aim is to encourage students to apply what they have learnt to their academic studies in English.

PROCEDURE

1 Students read the instructions. Encourage students to look at the *Language for Writing* on pp71–72. Students complete the task individually. Students compare answers with a partner. Ask one or two students who have drawn different graphs to draw their graph on the board.

This exercise could be set for homework and the students could present their graphs on PowerPoint if this is available. **⊙━ 1**

2 Students read the instructions. Encourage the students to look back at the *Language for Writing* on pp71–72. Students do the task individually and compare answers with a partner. Ask one or two students to read out their answers to the class. Students discuss which answer they like best. **⊙━ 2**

3 Students read the instructions and complete the task individually. Students compare answers in pairs. Elicit the answers. **⊙━ 3**

4 Students read the **Study Skill** and the instructions. Explain that sometimes when a suffix is added to the stem, a letter (vowel) may be lost, for example, *taste: tasty*. Students complete the task individually. Students compare answers in pairs. Elicit answers and ask the students what part of speech the word is. (They should recognize this from the suffix.) **⊙━ 4**

5 Students read the instructions and complete the task individually. Focus students' attention on the example which uses the stem word. Not all the answers can use the stem word in the definition. Encourage the students to use a dictionary if necessary. Elicit the answers. **⊙━ 5**

EXTENSION ACTIVITY

Ask the students to list the skills they have learnt and practised in this unit. For example:
– interpreting non-textual information
– describing visual information
– word-building

Put students into small groups to discuss how they could apply these skills to their academic studies.

⊙━ 1
Model answer

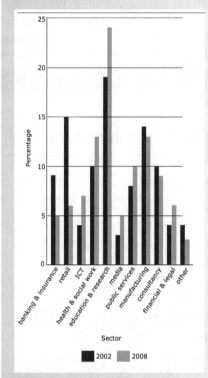

Table 5: Graduate employment destinations from Woodville University in 2002 and 2008 in percentages

⊙━ 2
Model Answer
The bar chart shows the sectors of employment chosen by graduates from Woodville University between 2002 and 2008. The biggest decreases were in the sectors of retail, where numbers dropped by around 50%. The largest increase was in education and research, which in 2008 employed one in four of all graduates. Other sectors which saw a rise in popularity were health and social work, the media, and ICT. One in ten of the graduates in 2008 went into public services. However, there was a substantial decrease in the numbers employed in banking and insurance and in retail, and the percentage of graduates who worked in manufacturing and consultancy declined slightly.

⊙━ 3

1 preset   2 kilogram   3 illegal   4 retake   5 monolingual

⊙━ 4

1 <u>un</u>comfortable	adjective
2 <u>in</u>accurately	adverb
3 <u>re</u>appearance	noun
4 <u>in</u>distinguishable	adjective
5 <u>inter</u>disciplinary	adjective

⊙━ 5

2 wrongly interpreted
3 translated and written at the bottom of the screen
4 related to each other
5 constructed again
6 very small processor

10 Communication and technology

READING SKILLS Dealing with longer texts (3) and (4)
LANGUAGE FOR SPEAKING Language for presentations
WRITING FOR SPEAKING How to be a good presenter • Preparing notes for a presentation • Giving a presentation
VOCABULARY DEVELOPMENT Formal and informal vocabulary

READING Communication technology pp76–78

AIMS

The aim of this section is to help students deal with longer texts more effectively by being decisive and selective about what and how to read.

LEAD IN

• Focus students' attention on the page. Ask students to identify the skill READING, and the topic (*Communication technology*)
• Ask:
  – *What ways do you use to communicate with people?* (telephone, mobile, SMS, email, etc.)
• Put students' ideas on the board.

PROCEDURE

1 Students read the instructions. Put students into pairs to discuss the questions. Ask the students for their ideas. Put these on the board. Students compare their answers from the lead in with their answers to question number 2. ⚷ 1

2 Students read the **Study Skill**. Emphasize the importance of reading a text with a purpose, that is, knowing what is required from the text, and then selecting those parts of the text that are important. Students read the instructions and complete the task. Students compare their answers in pairs.

   Write the list on the board and check the answers with the whole class. If there is disagreement, ask students to explain their answers. ⚷ 2

3 Students read the instructions and skim the text. Set a time limit of 60 seconds. Students check their predictions on the board. ⚷ 3

4 Students read the instructions and complete the task individually. Students compare answers in pairs. ⚷ 4

5 Students read the **Study Skill** and the instructions. Students work in pairs to complete the task individually. Write the partial notes on the board and ask students to complete them. The rest of the class compares their answers. ⚷ 5

6 Students read the instructions and complete the task individually. Remind students that they should go directly to the relevant paragraph (E) and not read other paragraphs. Write the notes on the board. Ask some students to come up and correct them. The rest of the class compares their answers. ⚷ 6

7 Students read the instructions and highlight the information they need to complete the notes. Students compare their selection in pairs. Students work individually to complete the notes. Ask a student to write their notes on the board. The rest of the class compares their answers. ⚷ 7

8 Students read the instructions. Remind students of the importance of thinking about and recalling what they have read. You may wish to ask students to shut their books. Write the questions on the board and ask students to answer the questions in pairs. Write their answers on the board. Students check their answers from the text and their notes. ⚷ 8

EXTENSION ACTIVITY

Tell students to read the text on pp76–77 again and to highlight new words and phrases. Students work in small groups and go through the text together, explaining their colleagues' words and phrases if they know them. Students should use a dictionary to look them up, and then record any remaining new vocabulary.

READING Answer key pp76–78

⚷ **1**
Possible answers
1 telegraph, pigeons, runners, etc.
2 telephone, mobile phone, SMS, emails, letters, videoconferencing, etc.
3 Students' own ideas.

⚷ **2**
Students' own answers.
As this is a prediction task, there is no 'right' or 'wrong' answer at this stage.

⚷ **3**

a carrier pigeons ✗	f radio ✓
b computers ✓	g telegraph ✓
c flags (semaphore) ✗	h telephones ✓
d mirrors ✗	i television ✓
e newspapers ✗	j typewriters ✗

⚷ **4** 1C 2G 3 J, K, L 4 P

⚷ **5**

1 Origins of electronic communication
   1.1 Invention of telegraphy 1830
   1.2 first practical telegraph 1838
   1.3 Historic examples of use
       1.3.i Krakatoa 1883
       1.3.ii sinking of Titanic 1912

⚷ **6**

2 The telephone
   2.1 Speech first transmitted 1867 1876
   2.2 Developments over 50 100 years
       2.2.i microphone added
       2.2.ii bell attached
       2.2.iii telephone book numbers created
       2.2.iv amplifiers added
   2.3 First long-distance phone calls 1920s

⚷ **7**

3 Mobile phones
   3.1 First generation (1G) 1980s
   3.2 **Second generation (2G)** 1990s
       3.2.i digital transmission
       3.2.ii **SMS added**
   3.3 **Second and a half generation (2.5G)**
       3.3.i WAP added
       3.3.ii **GPRS added**
       3.3.iii access to websites
       3.3.iv **coloured screens** and **cameras**
   3.4 **Third generation (3G) 2000**
       3.4.i new protocols led to **high-speed connections**

⚷ **8**

1 1980s   2 They had digital transmission and SMS.
3 They could access some websites.   4 2000
5 They led to high-speed connections.

LANGUAGE FOR SPEAKING
Language for presentations p79

AIMS
The aim of this section is help students to recognize and use fixed phrases and words that are commonly used in academic presentations.

PROCEDURE

1 Tell students to look at the photograph. Ask:
- *What is happening?* (A lecturer is giving a presentation)
- *Where is it happening?* (In a lecture theatre or seminar room)

Students read the instructions and complete the task. Students compare their answers in pairs. Write the headings on the board. Ask some students to come up and write in the sentences and phrases. The rest of the class check their answers. **⊙━1**

2 Students read the instructions and complete the task individually. Ask a student to read the introduction aloud. The rest of the class listens and checks their answers. **⊙━2**

3 Students look at the prompt card. Ask:
- *What is the presentation about?* (computer telephony)
- *How many parts is it divided into?* (four)

Students read the instructions and prepare the introduction to the presentation. It is better if students do not write full sentences; they should make notes with phrases to prompt them (see answers). **⊙━3**

4 Students read the instructions and practise giving the introduction to their presentation to their partner. Encourage them to listen attentively to their partner and to help with the correct use of the sentences and phrases.

Ask some students to give the introduction to the whole class.

⊙━1

Introduction
I'm going to talk about ...
My talk/lecture/paper is about ...
The subject of my talk/lecture/paper is ...
Structure
This talk will be divided into ... parts.
The first/second/next/last part ...
Next/Firstly/Secondly/Then/Finally I/we will look at/discuss ...
Clarifying/rephrasing
In other words, ...
... that is to say, ...
To put it another way, ...
Summarizing
To recap, ...
So, we have discussed ...
To summarize, ...
Changing subject
Now, let's turn to ...
Moving on, ...
Let's turn our attention to ...
Concluding
So, we have looked at ...
In conclusion, ...
To conclude, ...

⊙━2

Possible answers
1 I am going to talk about
2 This talk is divided
3 Firstly, I will
4 Next, I will describe
5 that is to say,
6 Finally,

⊙━3

Possible answer
Good morning, my talk is about computer telephony.
It is divided into four parts.
Firstly ... a description
Secondly ... the benefits to users
Next ... effects on landline network providers
And finally, ... effects on mobile phone network providers

WRITING FOR SPEAKING
Interpreting and translating pp80–81

AIMS
The aims of this section are to make students aware of the differences between a written and a spoken presentation, and to give them practice in the making of notes for a presentation.

PROCEDURE

1 Students read the **Study Skill**. You may wish to discuss other aspects of giving a presentation, e.g. making eye-contact with the audience, speaking at the right volume, etc.

Students read the instructions and complete the task. Students should work in pairs or small groups. Check the answers with the whole class. Ask students what features of the sentences allowed them to decide if they were more likely to be spoken or written English (use of the subject pronoun *I*, asking direct questions, repetition, etc. are all signs of spoken English). **⊙━1**

2 Students read the **Study Skill**. Ask:
– *Why is presenting from notes generally better than reading aloud?* (reading aloud can sound monotonous; if a text is written, there is no recapping, rephrasing, etc. so it is harder for the audience to follow)

Students read the instructions and complete the task individually. **⊙━2**

Do not explain *ad-hoc interpreting* at this stage. It is explained in exercise 5.

3 Students read the instructions and complete the task. Put students into pairs or small groups to present their introductions. Encourage students to give feedback to their partners. **⊙━3**

4 Students read the instructions and complete the task. Write the incomplete notes on the board. Ask some students to complete the notes. The rest of the class compare their answers. **⊙━4**

5 Students read the instructions and complete the task. Tell students to highlight the relevant information before making their notes. Students compare their prompt cards in pairs or small groups. **⊙━5**

Giving a presentation p81

6 This exercise could be set for homework. Students read the instructions. Tell students to think of a topic relating to their field of study on which they could give a short presentation (5–10 minutes).

Ask students to recall the difference between the language of spoken presentations and written language. (See Student's Book p80). This is especially important if students are preparing a presentation based on an essay.

If you have the facilities, students could give a PowerPoint presentation.

Rather than spend a whole class with the students giving their presentations, you may wish to draw up a timetable of when each student gives their presentation.

To exploit these presentations as much as possible, ask the rest of the class to ask the presenter questions, and to give the speaker some feedback at the end of the presentation on the way the presentation was given. For example: *Was the speaker loud enough/slow enough/clear enough? Did he or she rephrase/recap? Was the structure of the talk clear?*

EXTENSION ACTIVITY
If your students have access to a voice recorder or a ViaVoice computer program, tell them to record their presentation from exercise 6. Tell students to listen critically to their presentation:

– Was it the right length?
– Was it organized logically?
– Did they speak slowly and clearly enough?
– Did they cover all the main points?

WRITING FOR SPEAKING Answer key pp80–81

⊙━1
1 Good morning everyone. S
2 I would like to talk about university education in Singapore. S
3 This essay will explore the differences between dialects and accents. W
4 Firstly, I shall describe the development of video-conferencing in the 1990s. S
5 Let's turn our attention to why some countries do not teach a foreign language until secondary school. S
6 As will become clear below, other languages are now becoming much more commonly used on the Internet. W
7 Is everyone with me so far? S
8 Therefore, to summarize, the main arguments in favour of early language education are as follows. B
9 Are there any questions? S
10 Let me put that another way. S
11 In other words, English has become the main language of international trade and commerce. B
12 Let me recap the main points so far. S

⊙━2
1 interpreting
2 five main sections (introduction, qualifications, types of interpreting, situations for interpreting, conclusion)
4 simultaneous, consecutive, conference, ad-hoc

⊙━3
Students' own answers.

⊙━4
2 **What qualifications are needed?**
  2.1 Education i degree in interpreting
              ii degree in languages + **postgraduate training in interpreting**
  2.2 Languages i mastery of at least 1 foreign language
              ii know **country's institutions, culture, attitudes, and practices**
  2.3 **General knowledge** i broad
                          ii **up to date**

⊙━5
Possible answers
3 **Types of interpreting**
  3.1 Simultaneous interpreting
    3.1.i   from foreign into mother tongue
    3.1.ii from booth/small room directly or whispering translation directly
  3.2 Consecutive interpreting
    3.2 i   speaker pauses for interpreter
    3.2.ii interpreter takes notes
4 **Situations for interpreting**
  4.1 Conference interpreting
    4.1.i   very common
    4.1.ii   national/international
    4.1.iii meeting/informal gathering
  4.2 Ad-hoc interpreting
    4.2.i   a service for people who can't speak the language of the country they are in
    4.2.ii for health, legal, or education services

VOCABULARY DEVELOPMENT
Formal and informal vocabulary p82

AIMS

The aims of this section are to make students aware of the different levels of formality inherent in vocabulary, and to help them recognize and choose the correct level of formality for their written and spoken work.

LEAD IN

- Write these pairs of words and phrases on the board.

apologize	*say sorry*
investigate	*look into*
visit	*drop in*

- Ask:
  - *What is the difference between the words on the left and those on the right?* (the words on the left are just one word, the ones on the right are phrasal vocabulary)
- If you cannot elicit the terms *formal* and *informal* from the students, leave this until after exercise 1.

PROCEDURE

1 Students read the **Study Skill**. Tell students to look at the words on the board and again. Ask:
  - *Which verbs are more formal?* (verbs on the left)

Students read the instructions and complete the task individually. Students compare their answers in pairs. Check the answers with the whole class. Ask:
  - *Which sentences are more formal/more informal?*
  - *What language helped you choose the word?* 🔑 1

2 Students read the instructions. Tell students to first read the whole paragraph. Ask:
  - *When did the history of sign languages start?* (16th century CE)
  - *The gestures only represent words. True or False?* (False, they also represent ideas)
  - *All sign languages are the same. True or false?* (False, they vary from country to country, region to region)

Students complete the task, working individually, and then compare answers in pairs. Ask a student to read out their paragraph. The rest of the class listen and compare their answers. 🔑 2

3 Students read the instructions. Put students into pairs or small groups to discuss each sentence and to identify the more informal word or phrase.

Check the answers with the whole class. 🔑 3

4 Students read the instructions and complete the task individually. Students compare their answers in pairs. Ask some students to read out the sentences using the more formal words and phrases. The rest of the class listen and check their answers. 🔑 4

VOCABULARY DEVELOPMENT Answer key p82

🔑 1

1 estimates (the context is formal)
2 look like (the context is informal and other words in the sentence are informal, e.g. *phones, just don't, 60s*)
3 advisable (the context is formal and other words in the sentence are formal, e.g. *examination*)
4 widespread (the context is formal)
5 send (the context is informal and other words in the sentence are informal, e.g. *lots of*)
6 decrease (the context is formal and other words in the sentence are formal, e.g. *announced, rapidly*)

🔑 2

How can you (1) <u>communicate</u> your ideas to people if you (2) <u>are not able to</u> speak, perhaps because you are deaf? It would (3) <u>be very time-consuming</u> to write down everything you needed to (4) <u>express</u>. One solution is to use sign language. The recorded history of sign languages, (5) <u>that it to say</u>, languages using one's hands, began in the sixteenth century. The gestures used by signers can (6) <u>represent</u> complete ideas in addition to single words. (7) <u>In the same way as</u> spoken languages, signed languages vary from country to country and from region to region. (8) <u>As a result</u>, there is a wide variety of signed languages in use around the world.

🔑 3

1 For further information on courses in Communication Technology, <u>get in touch with</u> Dr Williams in the Department of Information Technology.
2 From 1950 to 2000 there were <u>very big</u> developments in the field of computer technology.
3 Please <u>let</u> the director <u>know</u> if there are any problems.
4 Students who <u>miss</u> classes as a result of illness are required to produce a medical certificate.
5 The director of the department will <u>get here</u> at 3pm.
6 All books must be <u>brought back</u> to the library by Monday 26th June.

🔑 4

b get here	c get in touch with	d very big
e brought back	f let … know	

REVIEW p83

AIMS

The aims of this section are to give students further practice in the skills learnt in this unit, and to give them the opportunity to review the work they have done. A further aim is to encourage students to apply what they have learnt to their academic studies in English.

PROCEDURE

1 Students read the instructions and complete the task. Ask a student to write the notes on the board. The rest of the class check their answers. **O⌐ 1**

2 This exercise can be set for homework. Students read the instructions. Remind them to prepare prompt cards and to use phrases from the *Language for Speaking* on p79.

Students may prefer to do a PowerPoint presentation.

Students can present their talks to the class, or in small groups. **O⌐ 2**

3 Students read the instructions and complete the task individually. Encourage them to make notes on any other vocabulary in the text which is new, or which they think will be useful. Remind them to record it appropriately.

Ask some students to read out their answers. The rest of the class check their answers. **O⌐ 3**

4 Students read the instructions and complete the task individually. Students compare their answers in pairs. **O⌐ 4**

ADDITIONAL PHOTOCOPIABLE ACTIVITY

Writing 10 Proof-reading and editing

REVIEW Answer key p83

O⌐ 1

1 What is it?
   1.1 Local area network (LAN)
   1.2 **high-frequency** radio signals
   1.3 **sends & receives data over short distances** (60m)
2 How does it work?
   2.1 uses radio waves
   2.2 computer adapter translates data into **radio signals**
   2.3 radio signals transmitted **via antenna**
   2.4 **wireless router** receives/decodes signal
   2.5 sent to the **Internet**
3 Advantages
   3.1 more data can be sent
   3.2 **multiple devices** can use connection at the same time
4 Developments
   4.1 hotspots in **airports, shops, libraries, hotels, etc.**
   4.2 cities can provide **low-cost Internet access**

O⌐ 2

Students' own answers.

O⌐ 3

RAM	Random Access Memory
PC	Personal Computer
1G	First generation
SMS	Short Message Service
WAP	Wireless Application Protocol
3G	Third generation
Mb	megabits
PDA	Personal Digital Assistant
OS	operating system
GPS	Global Positioning System

O⌐ 4

1 The new university hall can <u>fit in</u> (accommodate) 500 people.
2 Will all students <u>pick up</u> (collect) their essays from the secretary's office?
3 The director's meeting has been <u>put off</u> (postponed) until next week.
4 We are pleased to announce that Dr Smith has <u>got over</u> (recovered from) his recent illness and will be returning to the university next week.
5 All new students must <u>fill in</u> (complete) their library membership forms by the end of this week.

Writing 1 Comparing and contrasting

1 Read the information in the table. Match the sentences on the left with their equivalents on the right.

Example: 1c

SCHOOL	UNIVERSITY
1 ☐ The school year is divided into three terms.	a Students are responsible for their own time management.
2 ☐ Most learning takes place in the classroom.	b There is a timetable, but is often more varied and flexible, and attendance for some classes can be optional.
3 ☐ Time is arranged and organised for students.	c The academic year usually consists of two semesters.
4 ☐ There is a fixed class timetable and attendance is compulsory.	d Students generally have less access to academic staff, and feedback is less frequent.
5 ☐ Class sizes are usually limited to around thirty students.	e Students are encouraged to develop critical and analytical thinking skills when dealing with new information.
6 ☐ Students generally learn factual information which they are not required to analyse in great depth.	f Some teaching takes place face-to-face with a teacher, but students also learn through lectures, seminars, computer-based or online learning, and laboratory or field work.
7 ☐ There are limited types of assessment, mainly in-class exams.	g There are varied types of assessment, for example course work, project work, presentations and take-home exams as well as in-class exams.
8 ☐ Students have frequent access to their teachers, and receive constant feedback on their progress.	h Class sizes can be very large, with some lectures attended by over one hundred students.
9 ☐ Teaching is usually face-to-face with the teacher in the classroom.	i Some learning takes place in classes, but students are expected to do a lot of independent learning and study.

2 Write sentences to link the sentences in exercise 1, using the expressions for expressing similarity and difference.

LANGUAGE BOX
Similarity: In the same way, … / … is/are similar in that …
Difference: … whereas … / On the other hand, / In contrast, / … is/are different in that …

Example: The school year is divided into three terms. *In contrast*, the academic year usually consists of two semesters.

3 Think of other differences between life at school and life at university, using the following prompts:
- living at home / away from home
- food & cooking
- budgeting.

Example: School students either live at home or in a boarding school. *On the other hand*, in the United Kingdom most university students live in university accommodation or shared houses

4 Now organise all your sentences in exercises 2 and 3 into topic paragraphs and add your sentences from Exercise 3 to make the following essay: *Compare and contrast student life at school and at university* (150 words).

Writing 2 Rephrasing

1 Skim the text for 1 minute. What is the topic?

2 Match the topic sentences to the paragraphs.

---

a What researchers have been able to do, however, is to identify some of the daytime problems that people who have trouble sleeping suffer from.

b Insomnia is typically defined as an inability to fall asleep, or as chronic sleeplessness.

c Can medicines help a person to be able to overcome the problem of insomnia?

d A much better treatment for insomnia is a natural one.

e The problem with insomnia research is the fact that there are many different factors that can cause insomnia.

---

1 ☐ In fact, it is a sleeping **disorder** that is shown by a patient's inability to fall asleep or to stay asleep for a period of time that is necessary. Specialists have recognized three main types of **insomnia**. These are short-term insomnia, which is simple sleeplessness that only last for a night or so, chronic insomnia, where a patient has a difficult time falling asleep nightly for a month or more, and acute insomnia, where a patient will not sleep well for three weeks to six months. Because insomnia is such a **widespread** problem, insomnia research is **ongoing** in order to find a cure.

2 ☐ These range from drinking too much caffeine to stress and **anxiety** or even problems with the thyroid. Because of the wide **diversity** of causes that could bring on insomnia, it is difficult to find a cure for the disease.

3 ☐ These problems can include a person being unable to **concentrate** or do simple problem-solving to feeling dizzy. Other problems include a general feeling of tiredness during the day, **reduced** energy levels, blurred vision, and **irritability**.

4 ☐ Although doctors will be able to prescribe some medicine, the problem is that many of these medications will not help insomnia sufferers to sleep well, they will simply help them to be unconscious during the night. Many people also feel that these medications prevent them from going through the proper sleep cycles in order for their sleep to be considered good.

5 ☐ If sufferers do not have an underlying medical cause which would necessitate medical attention, they can treat their insomnia by one of the following natural **means**. They can get some exercise in the early afternoon in order to tire their body out for the evening's rest. About an hour before bedtime, they can turn off the TV and try not to do anything mentally stimulating until it is time for bed. They can also take a warm bath and enjoy some relaxing music to prepare their mind for sleep.

---

3 Match the words in the left column with their near synonyms in the right column

1 widespread	a sleeplessness	6 reduced	f worry
2 concentrate	b very common	7 irritability	g bad temper
3 disorder	c variety	8 anxiety	h decreased
4 diversity	d think clearly	9 ongoing	i methods
5 insomnia	e problem / illness	10 means	j continuing

4 Look at the sentences below. Replace the underlined words with suitable near synonyms from exercise 3.

       sleeplessness

1 Research into <u>insomnia</u> is <u>ongoing</u> because it is a <u>widespread</u> <u>disorder</u>.

2 Insomnia has a wide <u>diversity</u> of causes, ranging from <u>anxiety</u> to caffeine.

3 During the day, insomnia sufferers can experience <u>reduced</u> energy levels, <u>irritability</u>, and difficulties when trying to <u>concentrate.</u>

4 Natural <u>means</u> of treating insomnia, such as taking exercise, are considered preferable to prescribed medicines.

5 Write a paragraph (80–100 words), using some of the expressions in exercise 4, to summarise the main ideas in the article.

1 You are planning to write an article for a community magazine to persuade the readers to improve facilities for cyclists in your city. Think of as many ideas about the environmental and health benefits of cycling as you can, and write them down.

2 Look at the information below about cycling in large cities, and see if any of your ideas are included. Then organize the information into topic categories.

Cycling equipment	Cycling facilities	Speed & convenience of travel	Environment	Health & safety

1 a network of cycle lanes covering the whole city

2 cycling provides good aerobic exercise

3 travelling by bicycle instead of by car decreases the amount of air pollution

4 many bicycle parking facilities

5 a bicycle hire system

6 travelling by bicycle reduces traffic noise

7 cycle lanes need to be maintained and kept safe

8 special traffic lights for cyclists

9 cyclists avoid traffic jams and delays

10 a company scheme to help employees buy bicycles

11 cycling in cities is often faster than driving

12 roadside bicycle repair and service centres throughout the city

13 cycling in cities can be dangerous

14 cycling equipment is expensive

15 after the initial expenditure, cycling is a much cheaper method of transport

16 cycling is a good way of discovering nature

17 cyclists need to do a cycling awareness course

18 cycling helps protect green spaces from pollution

19 public transport by train is faster and more comfortable

20 travelling time is easier to predict when cycling

3 Go through the notes in the categories in exercise 2, and select the information which is relevant for your essay. Which piece of information in each category will you NOT use?

4 Write your magazine article on *The benefits of cycling in the city* (300 words), saying how and why your city should improve cycling facilities. Include relevant information only from exercises 1, 2 and 3.

1 Discuss the following questions in pairs

- What is a carbon footprint?
- Why is it important to reduce our carbon footprint?
- How can we as individuals reduce our carbon footprint?

2 Read the suggestions below.

a Do they include any of your ideas?

b Rephrase the sentences making compound adjectives by combining the underlined words:

1 When buying a car we can choose a model which uses <u>fuel</u> <u>efficiently</u>.

   Example: When buying a car we can choose a <u>fuel-efficient</u> model

2 We can try to be less <u>dependent</u> on <u>cars</u> by walking and using public transport

_____

3 We can cycle more as bicycles <u>save</u> <u>time</u> and are good for our health.

_____

4 We can buy fruit and vegetables which are <u>grown</u> <u>locally</u>.

_____

5 We can take measures which <u>save</u> <u>energy</u>, such as turning down our central heating.

_____

6 We can buy products that use packaging which is <u>friendly</u> to the <u>environment</u>.

_____

3 Read the essay title below and underline the key words. Plan an introduction to the essay.

The need to reduce environmental pollution and to conserve energy has become a major world issue. Describe three ways in which individuals reduce their carbon footprint.

4 Compare your plan with the one below:

- Energy conservation very important – world running out of resources + damage to the environment
- Individuals can play a role
- Explain 'carbon footprint'
- Thesis statement

5 Read this sample essay and write a conclusion to it (50–80 words).

It is becoming increasingly necessary to reduce environmental pollution and to conserve energy because the Earth is running out of natural resources, such as oil and gas. As a result, governments are under pressure to reduce their carbon emissions. It is clear that individuals can also try to reduce their carbon footprint - that is the amount of carbon dioxide emitted in their daily life. This essay will describe three ways in which individuals can reduce their carbon footprint.

First, every person can reduce their carbon footprint if they try to be less car-dependent. For instance, when they travel to work they can use public transport, such as buses or trains, or they can walk if they live quite near their work. Cycling is another time-saving way of travelling to work, and it also provides healthy exercise.

A second way in which individuals can reduce their carbon footprint is to try to save energy within the home. For example, they can do this by turning down their central heating in the winter, and they can switch off electrical equipment when they are not using it. They can also wash their clothes at a lower temperature, and hang their clothes to dry on a washing-line, instead of using a tumble-dryer. All these measures reduce the amount of electricity used.

A final way to reduce one's carbon footprint is to buy products which use environmentally-friendly packaging which can be easily recycled. For instance, it is better to buy drinks in glass bottles instead of plastic bottles because glass can be recycled.

To summarize,

1 Underline the key words in the following essay title: *Globalization has more positive than negative effects on culture and society*. To what extent do you agree or disagree?

2 Read the sentences below.
   a Decide if you agree or disagree with the statements.

   1 Globalization is helping countries to develop economically.

   2 There is a greater exchange of ideas between countries.

   3 People are losing their traditional customs and values.

   4 There is less difference between cultures.

   5 Countries become richer because they absorb a wider range of elements from different cultures.

   6 Young people throughout the world share the same youth culture.

   7 People throughout the world watch the same television programmes.

   8 Globalization is enabling more people to have a better education.

   b Note down reasons and /or examples to support your opinion.

   c Compare your answers in groups.

3 Rewrite the sentences in exercise 2, making them more <u>certain</u> or <u>uncertain</u>.
   a Use modal verbs and adjectives and adverbs of certainty and uncertainty.
   b Add a sentence giving a <u>reason</u> or <u>example</u> to support this opinion. Use words from the box below.

Language for expressing caution	
Modal verbs	may, might, could
Adjectives	(it is) certain, clear, probable, likely, possible, (it is) unlikely
Adverbs	certainly, clearly, probably, possibly
Language for giving examples and reasons	
Examples	For instance, For example,
Reasons	(This is) because of + *noun*, because + *clause*,

Example: Globalization may be helping countries to develop economically. *For instance*, Britain now imports a wide range of foodstuff from African countries.

5 For each of your points from exercise 2 think of the opposite opinion and write a third sentence for each on.
   a Start with *However*, or *On the other hand*,.
   b Add a sentence giving a reason or example to support this opinion.

Example: Sentence 1
Globalization may be helping countries to develop economically. *For instance*, Britain now imports a wide range of foodstuff from African countries. *However*, it would appear that poor farmers in developing countries may not be benefiting from this trade. This is *because* they may be producing less food for their own country.

Writing 6 Indicating reason and result

1 Quickly scan this description of the history and main features of the Temple of Luxor in Egypt, and answer the following the questions:

a What was the main purpose of the temple?

b What happened to the temple after the 3rd century CE?

c Who rediscovered the temple?

d How high is the obelisk?

2 Re-read the text more slowly, focusing on the 16 verb choices in italics. Choose the correct form, <u>active</u> or <u>passive</u>, and underline the correct verb form. The first one has been done for you.

This essay will provide a short account of the history of Luxor Temple, which is one of the most important historical sites in the Nile Valley, Egypt. It will also **(1)** _describe_ / _be described_ some of the most important features of the temple.

Luxor Temple is located in the centre of the town of Luxor and **(2)** _dominates_ / _is dominated_ the banks of the Nile. It **(3)** _considers_ / _is considered_ to be an excellent example of Pharaonic temple architecture. It **(4)** _built_ / _was built_ by the pharaoh Amenthorp III, who was king during the period 1390-1353 BCE, and it was dedicated to Amon-Re, king of the gods, his wife Mut, and their son, Khons. Its main purpose was originally to celebrate the festival of Opet, and later it **(5)** _used_ / _was used_ as a place of worship for Christians and then Muslims.

Many rulers, such as Ramses II, **(6)** _continued_ / _was continued_ to add to the temple, and it was also further modified by Alexander the Great. In the 3rd century CE the temple **(7)** _occupied_ / _was occupied_ by Roman soldiers, and subsequently the site **(8)** _abandoned_ / _was abandoned_. Over the following centuries it became covered in sand and silt, and a village **(9)** _built_ / _was built_ within the temple walls. In fact, the temple remained buried for thousands of years under streets and houses.

Then in 1881 the archaeologist Gaston Maspero **(10)** _rediscovered_ / _was rediscovered_ the temple in remarkably good condition. However, before excavation work could begin the village had to **(11)** _remove_ / _be removed_. Only the mosque, which **(12)** _built_ / _was built_ in the 13th century CE on top of the remains of an early Christian church, was left intact and is still there today.

The temple **(13)** _approaches_ / _is approached_ by an impressive avenue of sphinxes which once stretched almost 2 kilometres from Luxor to Karnak. This avenue was built because statues of Amon-Re and his family **(14)** _carried_ / _were carried_ to Karnak during the Opet festival. Other important features are the two enormous seated statues of Ramses II and a pink granite obelisk, measuring 25 metres in height, which **(15)** _position_ / _are positioned_ at the entrance to the temple.

To sum up, the Temple of Luxor has a long and varied history and **(16)** _includes_ / _is included_ many impressive monuments. As a result, it is now considered one of the crowning glories of Egypt and is one of the most visited sites in the Nile Valley.

---

3 Basing your answers on the information in the text, match the sentence beginnings with their logical endings using words or expressions for reasons or results Use each linker once only.

Example: The Temple of Luxor was built in order to celebrate the festival of Opet.

1 The Temple of Luxor was built	because	**a** it became covered in silt and sand.
2 Many people visit the temple	in order to	**b** the avenue of sphinxes.
3 The Temple was abandoned.	because of	**c** celebrate the festival of Opet.
4 The approach to the temple is impressive	Consequently,	**d** statues of the gods could be carried to Karnak.
5 There was a village on top of the temple.	As a result,	**e** it is one of the most famous sites in the Nile Valley
6 The avenue of sphinxes was built	so that	**f** excavation work could not start immediately.

4 Write 6 sentences about places worth visiting in your country, giving either a reason or result and using an appropriate linker.

Example: Rome is famous _because of_ its many ancient monuments such as the Colosseum./ Visitors come to Rome _in order to_ see its buildings

1 Read the article on the Burj Khalifa and check the meaning of the following in your dictionary:
spire, reflective, recreational facilities, enable, inaugeration, residential, sky lobby.

Measuring 828 metres in height and **situated** on a man-made lake, the Dubai Burj Khalifa is now the tallest building in the world. At almost twice the height of the Empire State Building in New York, **which** measured 443 metres, **its** top spire can be seen from 95 kilometres away. **It** also has Y-shaped floor plan which aims to maximize the views of the Gulf. Until **its** inauguration in 2010, the tallest building was the Petronas Towers in Kuala Lumpur.

Designed by the architectural partnership Skidmore, Owings & Merrill, this impressive skyscraper has 162 floors, of **which** 49 are office floors. However, it was also built for residential purposes, and it houses 1044 apartments. **This** makes it highly original as it is the first tower to be built for this purpose. In fact, it is estimated that around 12,000 people will live and work in the tower when it is fully occupied. The building also has a public observation deck, sky lobbies with swimming pools, recreational facilities such as spas and fitness centres, and the highest mosque in the world. Other impressive features are **its** 3,000 underground parking spaces and 54 elevators which can reach speeds of 65 km per hour, travelling from ground level to the top floor in one minute.

Construction of the Burj Khalifa started in 2004 and was completed in January 2010, with an estimated 12,000 workers on site during construction. Over 330,000 cubic meters of concrete and 31,400 metric tonnes of steel were used to complete the tower. **Its** exterior, which is designed to withstand Dubai's extreme summer temperatures, is covered by 28, 261 reflective glass panels. Each one of **these** was cut by hand and installed by Chinese specialists. The water collected from the tower's air conditioning system totals 15,000 litres per year and **it** is to be used for garden irrigation.

---

2 Read the article again and identify the words which the words in **bold** refer back to.

3 Read the article again and find 3 main ideas. Which of these ideas does the article include?

a) The views from the Burj Khalifa	**d)** Internal features of the Burj Khalifa
b) Location & dimensions of the Burj Khalifa	**e)** Materials and construction of the Burj Khalifa
c) The cost of building the Burj Khalifa	

4 Write a summary of 100–120 words of the text, using the verbs for reporting another writer's ideas from the box below:

describe	explain	argue	believe	claim	report

Example: In this article the author *describes* the Burj Khalifa.

1 Do the quiz below, then check your answers by doing some research on the Internet. Work with a partner. Discuss where to find the answers and make a note of the sites and sources you use.

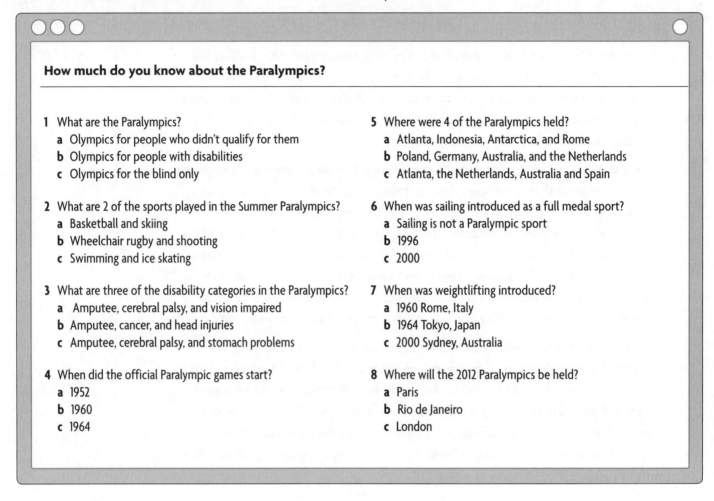

How much do you know about the Paralympics?

1 What are the Paralympics?
   a Olympics for people who didn't qualify for them
   b Olympics for people with disabilities
   c Olympics for the blind only

2 What are 2 of the sports played in the Summer Paralympics?
   a Basketball and skiing
   b Wheelchair rugby and shooting
   c Swimming and ice skating

3 What are three of the disability categories in the Paralympics?
   a Amputee, cerebral palsy, and vision impaired
   b Amputee, cancer, and head injuries
   c Amputee, cerebral palsy, and stomach problems

4 When did the official Paralympic games start?
   a 1952
   b 1960
   c 1964

5 Where were 4 of the Paralympics held?
   a Atlanta, Indonesia, Antarctica, and Rome
   b Poland, Germany, Australia, and the Netherlands
   c Atlanta, the Netherlands, Australia and Spain

6 When was sailing introduced as a full medal sport?
   a Sailing is not a Paralympic sport
   b 1996
   c 2000

7 When was weightlifting introduced?
   a 1960 Rome, Italy
   b 1964 Tokyo, Japan
   c 2000 Sydney, Australia

8 Where will the 2012 Paralympics be held?
   a Paris
   b Rio de Janeiro
   c London

2 Below are some comments about the Paralympics. Rewrite them following the example given. You will need to include punctuation and capital letters. The first one has been done for you.

1 Lewis 2010 claims the standards seem to keep on getting higher p2

Example: Lewis (2010) claims that "the standards seem to keep on getting higher" (p2).

2 according to Brand 2008 it challenges the accepted view of what humans van do both mentally and physically p1

3 Carter 2008 states at the Paralympics the levels of performance have improved to such an extent that most ordinary people couldn't do what some of these athletes are able to achieve p25.

4 as a distance runner Philip Hunter 2004 explains the standards we set our athletes particularly in track events are becoming exceptional p35

3 Write a paragraph (60–80 words) introducing the Paralympics and presenting its positive points, using some of the comments from exercise 2.

STUDENT A

1 Write a description of the sales trends for the Glamwear Company for the year 2009.

2 Then dictate your sentences to Student B so that Student B can draw an accurate graph.

3 Student B will dictate his/her sentences. Draw the graph.

4 When you have both finished drawing your graphs, you can compare them with the originals.

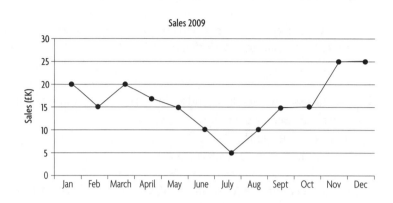

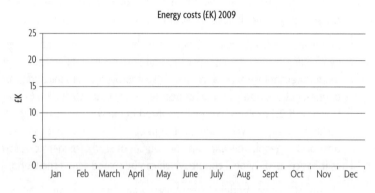

✂- -

STUDENT B

1 Write a description of the energy costs for the Compass Electrics company for the year 2009.

2 Student A will dictate his / her sentences. Draw the graph.

3 Then dictate your sentences to Student A so that Student A can draw an accurate graph.

4 When you have both finished drawing your graphs, you can compare them with the originals.

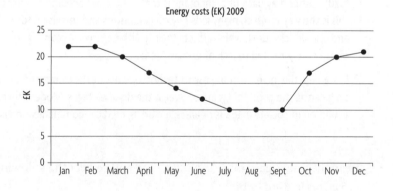

Writing 10 Proof-reading and editing

1 Read the essay title below and underline the key words.

> Although modern technological advances have brought benefits to society, they have also had a negative impact.
> To what extent do you agree with this view?

2 Read the essay written by a student, and answer the following questions.
- Does it answer the question?
- Is it well structured?
- Does it support points with comments from writers?

It is certainly true that developments in technological have greatly benefited society. However some people argue that modern technology have also had a negative impact on lifestyles and traditions. This essay will discusses both the advantages and disadvantages of modern technological advances.

In the one hand, it is clear that modern technology has many advantages. Firstly, it has greatly improved medicine by enabling more faster and more accurate diagnosis of illness and by making laser surgery possible. secondly, modern technological advances have also improved communication through the Internet and the use of mobile phones, but it is now possible for people to stay in touch and do business much more quick and efficiently. Downes (2007) explains 'Without the Internet many business transactions would take weeks' (p12). In fact, Wi-Fi technology is everywhere and most of people have got mobile phones. In contrast, the Internet has also made it possibly for people following on-line courses of study. Furthermore, satellite television has brought many benefits as it has created a global culture which can be shared across the world.

On the other side, modern technology has also brought some disadvantage. As Montague (2008) states: 'Local cultures are suffering from globalization, and this is destroying traditional customs in many parts of the world' (p20). Other drawback of technology is that people has become too dependent for technology. An example of this is the way in which many kids rely on computers and Television for entertainment. These children socialize less and also do less sport, which affects their health negative. According to Clifton (2009), 'the increase in childhood obesity is connected to lack of exercise' (p43).

In sum up, the increase in the use of technology has both advantages and disadvantages. However, I believe that, on balance, the good things are outweigh the disadvantages. Modern technology has clearly contributed for the evolution of society in loads of areas, including medical, communication and education. (325 words)

3 Read the essay again more carefully. Find and correct the following types of errors:
- 5 errors in word form
- 5 errors in verb forms or verb tenses
- 5 errors in grammar (prepositions, comparative forms etc)
- 5 errors in punctuation
- 5 errors in linking words
- 5 errors in style / register

4 Using the corrected essay as a model, write an essay (250–300 words) in answer to the following question.

'Technological advances in transport have brought many benefits to my country, but they have also had a negative effect on our quality of life'. To what extent do you agree with this view?

Teacher's Notes: Writing 1 and 2

1 Comparing and contrasting

AIM

To gain practice in the use of compare and contrast language; to compare and contrast student life at school and at university; to gain practice in writing a short academic compare & contrast essay.

This essay type is a useful preparation for IELTS Task 2 questions and for academic compare & contrast essays. It can be set as homework or done as an extension activity in class.

PROCEDURE

1 Photocopy one worksheet per student.
2 Elicit the differences between the expectations of school and university students.
3 Check vocabulary: *analytical/critical skills, assessment, attendance, compulsory/optional, feedback, field work, frequent, lecture, seminar.*
4 Students match information about school students with parallel information about university students. Students work individually, then compare answers in pairs/small groups.
5 Students link the matched pieces of information from exercise 1 using the compare & contrast language in the box. Students can work alone or in pairs.
6 Working in pairs or small groups, students add their own ideas.
7 Students organise their linked sentences thematically into paragraphs. This can be done in pairs / small groups in class or set as homework. Students then write their own essays individually.

ANSWERS

1 1 c; 2 i; 3 a; 4 b; 5 h; 6 e; 7 g; 8 d; 9 f.
2 **Possible answers**
   1 The school year is divided into three terms. **In contrast,** the university academic year usually consists of two semesters.
   2 At school most learning takes place in the classroom, **whereas** at university students are also expected to do a lot of independent learning and study.
   3 Time is arranged and organised for school students. **In contrast,** university students are responsible for their own time management.
   4 At school there is a fixed class timetable and attendance is compulsory. **On the other hand,** the university timetable is often more varied and flexible, and attendance for some classes can be optional.
   5 Class sizes are **different in that** in schools they are usually smaller / limited to around thirty students (and in university there can be one hundred students in a class).
   6 School students generally learn factual information which they are not required to analyse in great depth. **In contrast,** university students are encouraged to develop critical and analytical thinking skills when dealing with new information.
   7 At school there are limited types of assessment, mainly in-class exams. **On the other hand,** at university there are varied types of assessment, for example course work, project work, presentations and take-home exams as well as in-class exams.

8 School students have frequent access to their teachers, and receive constant feedback on their progress. **In contrast,** university students generally have less access to academic staff, and feedback is less frequent.
9 Teaching in school is usually face-to-face with the teacher in the classroom. **In the same way,** some teaching at university is face-to-face with a teacher, but it is **different in that** students also learn through lectures, seminars, computer-based or online learning, and laboratory or field work.
3 Students' own sentences.
4 Paragraphs could be organized according to the following topics: time management; class sizes; teacher contact; assessment; living independently; managing finances.

2 Rephrasing

AIM

To match topic sentences to paragraphs and to practise writing a paragraph using synonyms.

Summarising texts using their own words is an important academic writing skill; using a wide range of vocabulary and avoiding vocabulary repetition are also important for IELTS Writing Tasks 1 and 2.

PROCEDURE

1 Photocopy one worksheet per student.
2 Working alone then in pairs, comparing ideas, students review skimming a text for topic.
3 Working alone then comparing answers in pairs, students identify paragraph topics and match the topic sentences to the paragraphs.
4 Working alone, students do the synonym matching exercise.
5 Working in pairs, students use the words from exercise 3 as an aid to paraphrase.
6 Working alone students write a summary of the main ideas in the text using the synonyms. This exercise could be set as homework.

ANSWERS

1 The inability to sleep – definitions and possible cures
2 Paragraph 1 b; paragraph 2 e; paragraph 3 a; paragraph 4 c; paragraph 5 d.
3 1 b; 2 d; 3 e; 4 c; 5 a; 6 h; 7 g; 8 f; 9 j; 10 i.
4 Research into <u>sleeplessness</u> is <u>continuing</u> because it is a <u>very common problem</u>.

   Insomnia has a wide <u>range</u> of causes, ranging from <u>worry</u> to caffeine.

   During the day, insomnia sufferers can experience <u>decreased</u> energy levels, <u>bad temper</u>, and difficulties when trying to <u>think clearly.</u>

   Natural <u>methods</u> of treating insomnia, such as taking exercise, are considered preferable to prescribed medicines.

5 Possible answer:

> There are different degrees of insomnia, or sleeplessness, and it is a very common problem. It is difficult to research insomnia because it has a wide range of causes, ranging from worry to caffeine. During the day people who suffer from insomnia can experience decreased energy levels, bad temper, and difficulties when trying to think clearly. Although doctors can prescribe medicines to help sufferers sleep, many people are not satisfied with these methods. A better alternative is to use natural methods, for example taking exercise. (85 words)

3 Writing a persuasive article

AIM

To categorize and organize information for a persuasive article; to write a persuasive article.

Students should be familiar with the use of modal verbs *could* and *should* for proposing actions. Teachers could briefly check this when setting the task, and model some example sentences, e.g. *My city could build cycle paths where people could cycle safely / My city should provide free bicycles to encourage cycling.*

This writing task provides useful practice in presenting arguments and providing recommendations – skills which are required in both academic essays and IELTS Task 2 essays.

PROCEDURE

1 Photocopy one worksheet per student.
2 Working in pairs or small groups, students brainstorm ideas on the essay topic. The class shares their ideas.
3 Students work in pairs to categorize the information given. Teachers need to allow for some flexibility in some of the answers.
4 Students prioritize and select the information which they consider relevant. Students work alone then can compare in pairs or small groups. Some answers will depend on personal opinion.
5 Students write their own article, using the information provided and their own ideas. This could be set as homework.

ANSWERS

1 Students' own answers
2 & 3 (possibly exclude items in bold)

Cycling equipment	5. 10. **14**. 15
Cycling facilities	1. 4. **8**. 12.
Speed & convenience of travel	9. 11. **19**. 20
Environment	3. 6. **16**. 18
Health & safety	2. 7. **13** 17.

4 Possible answer:

The benefits of cycling in the city

Nowadays it is impossible not to be aware of the pollution caused by motor vehicles. The increase in the number of private cars has led rising traffic congestion, especially in large cities. At the same time people are becoming more concerned about remaining healthy and fit. As a result, travelling by bicycle has become popular in many large cities. Let's look at some of the main advantages of cycling in cities.

One of the benefits of cycling is that it improves the environment by reducing the amount of air and noise pollution in cities and by reducing the number of cars, so there are fewer traffic jams. In addition, cycling protects open green spaces, such as parks, from becoming polluted.

Cycling in cities is also more convenient and cheaper than using cars or public transport. Although many cyclists have to buy their own bicycle and cycling equipment, the cost of cycling is much cheaper than paying for public transport. It is easy for cyclists to predict the length of a journey because they can avoid traffic jams and use different routes.

There are many health benefits to be gained from cycling as it is a good way to get aerobic exercise and to keep fit. However, it is important for people who cycle in large cities to be safe. This means that cyclists may need to do a cycling awareness course and should wear safety helmets.

It is clearly the responsibility of the city council to make cycling more convenient, safer and more attractive by improving cycling facilities. Therefore the council should build more cycle lanes and make sure that these are well-maintained. The council could also provide more bicycle parking facilities and offer a roadside maintenance and repair service for cyclists. Cities like London and Paris now provide free bicycles for short trips within the city. If cities can't afford this, another way to encourage cycling would be to introduce a cheap cycle hire scheme.

All in all, cycling offers many benefits and solves some of the pollution and congestion problems in cities. It should therefore be encouraged and the city council should build all the necessary facilities. (359 words)

4 Writing introductions and conclusions

AIM

To practise planning and writing introductions and conclusions; to extend the topic of environmental protection to the contribution which can be made by individuals. The essay structure provides a good model for IELTS Task 2 essays, and the length is approximately that required for IELTS Task 2 (250+ words).

PROCEDURE

1 Photocopy one worksheet per student.

2 Students discuss the questions on the topic of *carbon footprint*.

A carbon footprint can be defined as *'a measure of the impact our activities have on the environment, and in particular climate change. It relates to the amount of greenhouse gases produced in our day-to-day lives through burning fossil fuels for electricity, heating and transportation etc.'* (http://www.carbonfootprint.com/carbonfootprint.html).

3 Students read possible suggestions and compare them with their own ideas in exercise 1.

4 Working in pairs, students rephrase the sentences by using compound adjectives.

5 Working alone, students identify key words in essay titles, and plan an introduction.

6 Students compare their plan for the Introduction with the one given.

7 Students study a sample essay on the topic and write a conclusion. The teacher should draw students' attention to more 'academic' style (e.g. topic sentences, clear signposting of each paragraph, no use of *we*, use of passive structures, use of the language of exemplification, etc.).

N.B. A good Conclusion should summarize the main points discussed in the essay. It should <u>not</u> introduce any new ideas or topics.

ANSWERS

2b 1. fuel-efficient, 2. car-dependent, 3. time-saving, 4. locally-grown, 5. energy-saving, 6. environmentally friendly.

When buying a car we can choose a <u>fuel-efficient</u> model

We can try to be less <u>car-dependent</u> by walking and using public transport.

We can cycle more as bicycles are <u>time-saving</u> and good for our health.

We can buy <u>locally grown</u> fruit and vegetables.

We can take <u>energy-saving</u> measures, such as turning down our central heating.

We can buy products that use <u>environmentally friendly</u> packaging.

3 The need to reduce environmental pollution and to conserve energy has become a major world issue. <u>Describe three ways</u> in which <u>individuals</u> <u>reduce their carbon footprint</u>.

5 Possible answer:

> To summarize, this essay has shown that individuals can reduce their carbon footprint in a number of different ways. Firstly, they can use their cars less frequently by choosing alternative forms of transport. Secondly, they can save energy in their homes by using less electrical equipment. Finally, they can buy goods which are packaged in recyclable materials. (56 words added – total = 318 words)

5 Giving reasons and examples

AIM

To practise giving reasons and examples to support opinions in academic and IELTS Task 2 essays

PROCEDURE

1 Photocopy one worksheet per student.

2 Working alone, students identify key words in the essay title.

3 Students read the statements and decide individually whether they agree or disagree with the statements. They then think of and note down reasons and examples to support their opinions.

4 Working in pairs / small groups, students exchange and discuss their opinions They use their reasons and examples to support their opinions. This will provide a basis for examining both sides of an issue in exercise 4.

5 Working in pairs, students rewrite the sentences in exercise 2 adding the language of caution and providing supporting evidence / examples from the box.

6 Working in pairs, or alone, or for homework, students practise all the points in the previous exercises in order to produce paragraphs incorporating *for* and *against* arguments and/or cause/effect. The focus of this exercise is to provide step-by-step practice in expressing *for* and *against* arguments supported with evidence / examples.

ANSWERS

1 & 2 Students' own views

3 All sentences should include expressions of un/certainty, exemplification.

4 Students' own sentences from Exercise 3, plus an additional sentence introduced by a linking word of concession – similar in structure to the paragraph given as an example

6 Indicating reason and result

AIM

To practise giving reasons and results in essays; to practise the use of passives in more formal academic writing. Descriptive writing incorporating all the features of academic writing studied in this unit are also useful for IELTS Task 2 essays.e.g. IELTS Task 2 essays.

Teacher's Notes: Writing 7 and 8

PROCEDURE

1 Photocopy one worksheet per student.

2 Check vocabulary: *temple, dominate, dedicated to, festival, modify, abandon, archaeologist, excavation, sphinx, obelisk.*

3 Students read the focus questions and scan the model descriptive essay for specific information. The essay provides a model for their own writing in exercise 4.

4 Students focus on language – active and passive verb forms. Working alone, students choose the correct verb form. They then compare their answers in pairs. The exercise can be considered as proof-reading practice, or the focus on active-passive forms can be used as either a consolidation or a diagnostic exercise, and could prompt the teacher to work on this in a remedial grammar slot.

5 Working alone, and then comparing in pairs, students select the appropriate reason or result linker to connect the sentence beginnings on the left to the reasons/results on the right. Students can refer back to the text to help them.

6 Students think of places worth visiting in their own countries. Students can brainstorm places in nationality groups. They can then write their descriptive essays individually or for homework.

ANSWERS

1 a) to celebrate the festival of Opet; b) the temple was abandoned; c) Gaston Maspero; d) 25 metres

2 (2)dominates, (3) is considered, (4) was built, (5) was used, (6) continued, (7) was occupied, (8) was abandoned, (9) was built, (10) rediscovered, (11) be removed, (12) was built, (13) is approached, (14) were carried, (15) are positioned, (16) includes.

3 1c, 2e, 3a, 4b, 5f, 6d

4 Students' own sentences.

7 Writing a summary

AIM

To identify then summarise main ideas using reporting verbs and focusing on the use of participles, pronouns and their referents. Effective use of participles and pronouns are an important element in fluent writing, and are necessary in both academic and IELTS writing. The use of reporting verbs is also needed in academic writing

PROCEDURE

1 Photocopy one worksheet per student.

2 Students read the article and gain practice in dictionary work. Working alone, students should try to work out the meaning of the words from context first, then check /look them up in their dictionaries.

3 Working alone, students identify the words/phrases which the words in bold refer to. Then they compare answers in pairs.

4 Working alone, then comparing in small groups, students identify the 3 main topics from the choices in the box. This is in preparation for the summarizing task in exercise 4.

5 Students summarize the main points and using the reporting verbs in the box. This can be done as collaborative writing in class, or can be set as homework.

ANSWERS

2 Paragraph 1: Measuring, situated, its, it, its = Burj Khalifa; which = Empire State Building; Paragraph 2: Designed = impressive skyscraper, which = 162 floors, this = all the previous sentence, its = the building; Paragraph 3: its = tower, these = glass cladding panels

3 Key topics: 1) b; 2) d; 3) e.

4 Possible summary using reporting verbs

> In this article the author describes the location and dimensions of the Dubai Burj Khalifa, which is currently the tallest building in the world. He states that this skyscraper has 162 floors and that it will be used for both offices and residential purposes. He reports / claims that the 54 elevators can take people from the bottom to the top floor in one minute. In the final part of the article, the author describes how the tower was built and explains how the reflective glass panels on the outside of the tower were made and how the water from condensation will be used for watering. (104 words)

8 Internet research task

AIM

To research information on the Internet; to write an essay using reporting verbs, incorporating quotations and following a referencing system. This task provides practice in using reporting verbs and incorporating research sources into an essay – essential academic writing skills. The essay type also provides useful practice for IELTS Task 2.

PROCEDURE

1 Photocopy one worksheet per student.

2 (The Quiz) the aim is to generate interest in the topic of Paralympics and to establish how much students know about the topic. The first question introduces the topic and can be discussed as a class. Students can then do the quiz in pairs, or alone then compare their answers in pairs. If they have access to the Internet, they can also do some research on the web. The teacher can provide the answers at the end of the task. Alternatively, the text below can be given or shown and students can find the answers.

3 Working alone and then comparing their answers, students practise crediting sources according to the guidelines in the Student's book, Unit 8, p63.

4 Working in pairs, students, write a paragraph, using the quotations from exercise 2.

5 Working alone, students write an essay for homework, which expands on their collaborative writing in exercise 3.

ANSWERS:

1 1B, 2B, 3A, 4B, 5C, 6C, 7 B, 8 B (2016) or C (2012) depending on date

Adapted from http://library.thinkquest.org/J0112424/takeourquiz.html

2 1 Lewis (2010) claims "the standards seem to keep on getting higher "(p.2).

2 According to Brand (2008), "it challenges the accepted view of what humans can do both mentally and physically" (p.1).

3 Carter (2008) states, "at the Paralympics the levels of performance have improved to such an extent that most ordinary people couldn't do what some of these athletes are able to achieve" (p.25).

4 As distance runner Philip Hunter (2004) explains, "The standards we set our athletes, particularly in track events, are exceptional" (p.35).

3 Possible answer: Sample paragraph incorporating quotations to support opinions.

> The Paralympics are an Olympic event created for disabled people, and they are expanding to include an increasing number of sports. Participants are now able to achieve very high levels of performance. According to Carter (2008), 'at the Paralympics the levels of performance have improved to such an extent that most ordinary people couldn't do what some of these athletes are able to achieve' (p.25). This view is supported by Lewis (2010) who claims that 'the standards seem to keep on getting higher' (p.2). These games clearly demonstrate that many disabled people can become very accomplished sportspeople. In fact, Brand (2008) states that the event 'challenges the accepted view of what humans can do mentally and physically' (p.1). (122 words)

POSSIBLE TEXT TO CHECK ANSWERS TO QUIZ

> The Paralympics is one of the most popular tournaments of the world, involving people with physical disabilities. This tournament is organized by the IOC (International Olympic Committee) and involves the participation of a large number of physically challenged sportspeople. These athletes include amputees, the visually impaired, and people who have cerebral palsy.
>
> The history of the Paralympics goes back to the years after the end of the Second World War. In 1948, a sports competition involving World War II soldiers with spinal cord injuries, was organized in Stoke Mandeville in England by Sir Ludwig Guttmann.

> The competition organized by Sir Guttmann gradually developed and culminated into the present Paralympic Games, a truly global event. A large number of athletes and players from different countries of the world participate in these games. The number of participant countries is on the rise, and from 23 in 1960 when the first games officially took place, the number has steadily grown, reaching 136 in the 2004. Some of the major sports which have been included in the Paralympic Games are: Ice Sledge Hockey, Swimming, Weightlifting, Cross Country and Alpine Skiing, Athletics and Shooting. Some sports have been included for many years; an example is Weight-lifting which was introduced in 1964. In contrast, other sports, for instance Sailing – introduced in 2000 – have become full-medal sports relatively recently.
>
> The Paralympics presents a chance to physically challenged people to showcase their sporting talents. It has come a long way since its early days and it has been held in locations as far apart as Atlanta, the Netherlands, Australia, and Spain. Currently, it is the second most popular sporting event in the world after the Olympics.

9 Describing graphs and trends

AIM

To provide an accurate description of information presented in a graph. To provide practice for IELTS Task 1. Students will be recycling the language of trends studied in Student's book, Unit 9, and should be using past simple forms of verbs. Teachers may wish to review these past forms first and also the use of prepositions (e.g. *rise to / by, drop from / to, over / during the next 3 months, in May*).

This is an information gap activity in which Student A and Student B have different graphs. The activity consists of three stages, plus a follow-up gap fill exercise using sample descriptions of the graphs. Students can work in A pairs and B pairs in the first stage, and then pair up, 1 A & 1 B student for the second and third stages. Teachers need to point out to students that the beginning of the months is on the left of the box. This will help students when drawing.

PROCEDURE

1 Photocopy one worksheet per pair of students.

2 Divided the class into two halves: A and B. As on one side of the room, and Bs on the other side of the room.

3 All students A are given the 'Student A' graph, and all students B are given the 'Student B' graph. Students (or student pairs) write descriptions of their graph.

4 Each Student A pairs up with a Student B. Students must not show each other either their drawing or their written text. Students A & B use the blank graph for this activity. This is the dictation stage, and it provides useful speaking practice studied in Student's book, Unit 9, p.71, and will need to focus on accuracy so that their partner can draw the graph correctly. The activity works best if Students A & B complete the dictation of both graphs before they compare their drawings.

5 The A + B student pairs compare their drawings with the originals. This enables them to locate any areas where there was misunderstanding of their partner's description, or where the description was misleading.

6 Students read a sample description of one of the graphs, and complete the missing prepositions.

7 Gapped text for students for extra practice.

The company's energy costs were £22, 000 (1) _____ the beginning (2) _____ January. They remained the same until the middle (3) _____ February. They then decreased steadily (4) _____ the next five months, reaching a low (5) _____ £10,000 (6) _____ the middle (7) _____ July. Energy costs levelled out (8) _____ £10, 000 until the middle (9) _____ September. Then there was a sharp increase (10) _____ £7,000 (11) _____ £17,000 (12) _____ mid-October and energy costs continued to rise, reaching £20,000 (13) _____ November. They increased (14) _____ £1,000 (15) _____ the following month, so they reached £21,000 (16) _____ December.

ANSWERS

1 at, 2 of, 3 of, 4 over/during/in, 5 of, 6 in, 7 of, 8 at, 9 of, 10 to, 11 in, 12 in, 13 in, 14 by, 15 in/during/over, 16 in

10 Proof-reading and editing

AIM
To review areas covered in the previous units of RP. To provide a final IELTS-Task 2 type writing task. This could be set as homework or as an exit test.

PROCEDURE

1 Photocopy one worksheet per student.

2 Working alone, students identify the key words in an essay question.

3 Students assess a student answer to the essay question in terms of structure and content.

4 Students read the essay again and proof-read it for language and register errors. The task could be divided up within a group of 6. Each student could peer teach the points in their category.

5 Students write their own essays on a similar topic.

ANSWERS

1 Key words: technological advances / benefits to society / negative impact / to what extent / agree

2 Yes to all questions. The essay is a good model in these respects.

3 Mistakes in bold.

It is certainly true that developments in **technology** have greatly benefited society. **However**, some people argue that modern technology **has** also had a negative impact on lifestyles and traditions. This essay **will discuss** both the advantages and disadvantages of modern technological advances.

On the one hand, it is clear that modern technology has many advantages. Firstly, it has greatly improved medicine by enabling ~~more~~ faster and more accurate diagnosis of illness and by making laser surgery possible. **Secondly**, modern technological advances have also improved communication through the Internet and the use of mobile phones, **and** it is now possible for people to stay in touch and do business much more **quickly** and efficiently. Downes (2007) explains 'Without the Internet many business transactions would take weeks' (p. 12). In fact, Wi-Fi technology is **widely available** ~~everywhere~~ and most ~~of~~ people **have** ~~got~~ mobile phones. In **additon**, the Internet has also made it **possible** for people **to follow** on-line courses of study. Furthermore, satellite television has brought many benefits as it has created a global culture which can be shared across the **world**.

On the other **hand**, modern technology has also brought some **disadvantages**. As Montague (2008) states: '**local** cultures are suffering from globalization, and this is destroying traditional customs in many parts of the world'. **Another** drawback of technology is that people **have** become too dependent **on** technology. An example of this is the way in which many **young people** ~~kids~~ rely on computers and **television** for entertainment. These children socialize less and also do less sport, which affects their health **negatively**. According to Clifton (2009), 'the increase in childhood obesity is connected to lack of exercise' (p. 43).

To sum up, the increase in the use of technology has both advantages and disadvantages. However, I believe that, on balance, the **advantages** ~~good things are~~ outweigh the disadvantages. Modern technology has clearly contributed for the evolution of society in **many** areas, including **medicine**, communication and education.

4 Students' own essays.